Tastes
& Tales

From A Distant Homeland

Enjoy

Alan and Katherine Strang

alan@thebrandforumltd.com

Tastes & Tales

From A Distant Homeland

© 2019 Meze Publishing Ltd.
All rights reserved.
First edition printed in 2019 in the UK.
ISBN: 978-1-910863-59-6
Written by: Alan and Katherine Strang
Photography: Katherine Strang
Edited by: Phil Turner, Katie Fisher
Cover by: Holly Furness
Designed by: Holly Furness
Printed in Great Britain by Bell and Bain Ltd, Glasgow

Published by Meze Publishing Limited
Unit 1b, 2 Kelham Square
Kelham Riverside
Sheffield S3 8SD

Web: www.mezepublishing.co.uk
Telephone: 0114 275 7709
Email: info@mezepublishing.co.uk

Tastes & Tales

From A Distant Homeland

Within this book are a selection of
'Tastes and Tales' from around the world,
all mixed together in one big pot.

Tastes from refugees' homelands:
the recipes are simple, and wherever
possible we have tried to make them in
one big pot to bring to the table
and share.

Tales to give an understanding of just
how hard others' lives can be and inspire
us all to help in whatever way we can.

Enjoy the pleasure of sharing dishes
with family and friends, and mix them
all together with love to create...

One Big Happy Pot!

It has been an incredible privilege to have met so many wonderful people during our time working as volunteers for Refugee Support, the charity set up by John Sloan and Paul Hutchings whose vision was to provide refugees not just with help and support but 'aid with dignity'.

Refugee Support touches everyone who is prepared to open their heart to the plight of fellow humans.

The inspiration for this book came when we were helping in the shop in Katsikas. It was fascinating to see how the ingredients that people chose from the limited selection on offer was so different from one culture to the next. We started to ask them what they were going to cook and then about the foods they cooked and missed from their homelands.

Inspired by our discussion, and the feeling that nothing is better than sharing stories over a big pot of food made with love, the idea for this book was born.

Hopefully everything will taste so much sweeter knowing that all the proceeds from this book will go to Refugee Support

to help continue to provide 'aid with dignity' to people whose lives have been devastated, just by being born in the wrong part of the world.

Tastes & Tales has been created from the heart, with every recipe prepared and photographed at home in our own kitchen, so please forgive us if any of the images are not as highly polished as those in some other foody books!

After 35 years of running a business in the fashion industry, Alan and Katherine Strang are now spending most of their time on the 220 Challenge they set up in 2014. The idea behind the 220 Challenge is to do as many acts of kindness as possible alongside supporting numerous charities, including Mary's Meals, Let's Feed Brum, Fight Hunger Foundation, Cancer Research and of course Refugee Support, to whom this book is dedicated.

A massive thank you to Holly Furness, an absolute superstar who has brought our vision for this project to life with her creativity and hard work.

CONTENTS

Starters and Mezze 6-37

Light Meals and Sides 38-77

Main Courses, Spices and Sauces 78-165

Puddings and Cakes 166-189

"If you have the
power to make
someone happy
today, do it.
The world needs
more of that."

Beetroot Yoghurt Dip

INGREDIENTS

Serves 4
1 cooked beetroot
3 tbsp extra-virgin olive oil
2 tbsp dried mint
1 clove of garlic, crushed
½ tsp salt
245g Greek yoghurt
½ tsp black pepper

METHOD

Grate the beetroot and then add 2 tablespoons of the olive oil, 1 tablespoon of the mint, the garlic and the salt. Mix everything together, leave to stand for 5 minutes, then fold in the yoghurt and black pepper.

When you are ready to serve the dip, swirl on the remaining tablespoon of olive oil and sprinkle with the remaining dried mint.

Delicious served as a dip with pitta bread, or any grilled meats and salad.

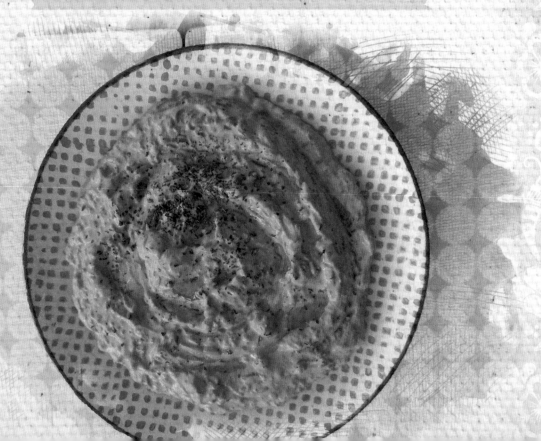

"The world will

not be destroyed by those

who do evil,

but by those who watch them

without doing anything."

Albert Einstein

Baba Ganoush

One of the most famous Middle Eastern recipes. We hope you like this version!

INGREDIENTS

Serves 4
- 3 aubergines
- 2 tbsp olive oil
- 2 cloves of garlic, roughly chopped
- 1 tbsp tahini
- 1 tsp ground cumin
- 2 lemons, juiced

METHOD

Preheat the oven to 180°c. Cut the aubergines in half straight down the middle and then score the flesh in a criss cross pattern (don't cut through to the skins).

Drizzle the aubergines with olive oil and pop in the oven on a baking sheet, with the fleshy part facing up. Cook for about 45 minutes or until soft, then take the aubergines out of the oven and leave to cool. Scoop the flesh out of the skins.

Pop the garlic in the food processor and blitz for 30 seconds.

Add the tahini, cumin, aubergine flesh, three quarters of the lemon juice and the olive oil.

Blitz until the baba ganoush is thick and smooth.

Tip into a bowl, drizzle with some extra-virgin olive oil and the remaining lemon juice then serve with flatbreads.

Muhammara
Syrian Red Pepper Dip

This dip can be used to jazz up your rice or added to a pasta sauce, and is also delicious served as a dip with raw veggies, breadsticks or crisps.

INGREDIENTS

Serves 4

- 6 red peppers
- 2 red chillies
- 50g breadcrumbs
- 2 cloves of garlic, crushed
- 2 tbsp lemon juice
- 1 tbsp balsamic vinegar
- 1 tsp salt
- 2 tsp ground cumin
- 2 tsp olive oil, plus extra for drizzling
- Black pepper (optional)
- Handful of walnut halves, finely chopped
- Fresh parsley, for decorating

METHOD

Preheat the oven to 200°c and put the peppers on a baking tray lined with foil. Bake for 30 to 40 minutes, turning occasionally, until the skins have blackened.

Pop the peppers in a bowl and cover with cling film. Leave for about 30 minutes until cool and then remove the skin, seeds and stem.

Put the peppers into a food processor along with all the other ingredients except the walnuts and parsley, then blend until smooth.

Stir in the walnuts, leaving a few to sprinkle over the top. Taste the dip to check the seasoning, then add more salt and black pepper if needed.

Tip the muhammara into a serving dish and sprinkle with the remaining walnuts, some chopped parsley and a drizzle of olive oil.

"If you **can't feed** a hundred **people** then just **feed one."**

Mother Teresa

Mast O Khiar
Persian Yoghurt Salad

Mast O Khiar is a cooling and creamy yoghurt dip infused with cucumber and herbs. This gorgeous dish is served on the side of most Persian meals, working brilliantly as a starter or served alongside kebabs and other sharing dishes.

INGREDIENTS

Serves 4
- ½ cucumber
- 250ml Greek yoghurt
- 1 clove of garlic, crushed or grated
- 3 spring onions, chopped
- 3 tsp chopped fresh mint
- 1 tsp dried mint
- Salt and pepper, to taste
- 1 tsp rose petals, for decoration

"Anger and intolerance can always be overturned with compassion."

METHOD

Coarsely grate the cucumber into a sieve and then use the back of a spoon to squeeze all the liquid out (you could also put the grated cucumber into a tea towel and squeeze all the liquid out that way).

Put the cucumber flesh into a large mixing bowl with all the ingredients, except for the rose petals and 1 teaspoon of fresh mint. Mix everything together and then taste the dip, adding salt and pepper as necessary.

When you are ready to serve, transfer the dip to a serving dish then sprinkle the rose petals and the remaining fresh mint over the top.

For a refugee, the possibility of beginning a
new life without fear is all they dream of.

"Every refugee carries a story of personal
pain and anguish. They share a common thread
of courage and determination to not only
survive and rebuild their shattered lives, but
to make a positive contribution to whatever
new community is prepared to accept them and
allow them to fulfil their true potential."

Discover
of the world
own

Experience diverse
cultures
your

Go on - try

the tastes
within your
kitchen.

flavours, aromas and
without leaving
front door

something new.

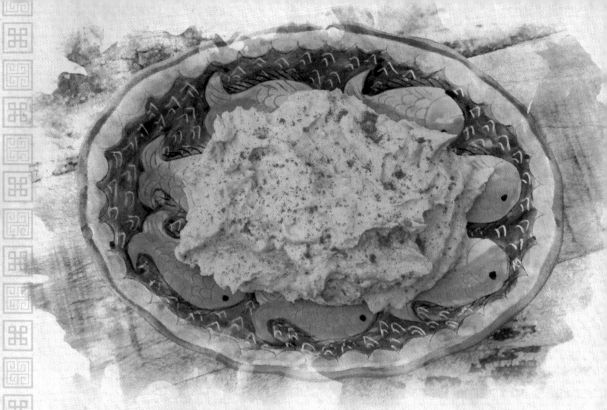

Happy Hummus

Hummus is served all over the Middle East, and what's not to love! It's so easy to make and fabulous for serving to a crowd of friends and loved ones: guaranteed to raise lots of smiles!

INGREDIENTS

Serves 4

- 3 tbsp tahini
- 1 lemon, juiced
- 400g tinned chickpeas
- 2 cloves of garlic, crushed
- 4 tbsp extra-virgin olive oil
- 1 tsp salt
- 1 tsp ground cumin
- 3 tbsp water
- Pinch of paprika

METHOD

Add the tahini and lemon juice to a food processor and blitz until thick for about 1 minute before adding the chickpeas. Process until smooth.

Add the garlic and blend while pouring in the olive oil a little at a time. Add the water until you get a consistency you like. You may need to add water if the mixture is quite thick.

Add the salt and cumin then pulse for 1 minute. Put the mixture into a serving dish and sprinkle on a little paprika.

Broad Bean Hummus

The combination of chickpeas
and broad beans is just heavenly,
and so simple to make.

INGREDIENTS

Serves 6

- 450g frozen broad beans, cooked and podded
- 150g tinned chickpeas
- 2 tbsp tahini
- 1 lemon, juiced
- 4 tbsp extra-virgin olive oil
- 2 cloves of garlic, crushed
- 1 tsp salt
- ½ tsp ground cumin
- 3 tbsp water
- Pinch of paprika

METHOD

Put all the ingredients except the olive oil and paprika in a food processor.

Blend until smooth, then slowly add the olive oil, pouring as a trickle.

If the mixture is too thick, add a little water.

Spoon into a serving dish and sprinkle over the paprika.

A Young Refugee from Syria

Now in refugee camp in Greece

My name is Ahmad, I am 19, Kurdish and from Syria. I left my country on my own 18 months ago. Before the war I went to school in Aleppo, played football, went to visit friends. Then the war started, so we left and went to Kobani for seven months.

I left Syria because I didn't know who to fight and I wanted a future. We just wanted freedom and then lots of new armies came. I would have to go to one of the armies because they have many armies there. Why fight? What for? I don't know who to fight for; maybe I would fight my brother. I can't do that.

If I fight I have to kill someone, and I don't want to kill anyone. And if I go to Isis they will kill me because I am Kurdish. Big countries made this war and we can't stop it.

I decided to go to Turkey and was there for about eight months before coming to Greece. My family want to travel but it is too expensive. Maybe 6,000 or 7,000 euros and they have no money. Now they must wait until the borders are opened.

I've always wanted to be a doctor. It was what my father wanted when he died ten years ago. I still want to be a doctor. When I was in Turkey I learnt Turkish but I can't stay there if I want to be a doctor. You just have to work.

I worked with iron but it was hard: 12 hours a day and they paid me half what other people get because I am a refugee. The journey was very difficult. The boat from Turkey to Greece was crazy, it took three hours at 2:00 in the morning. But I had to travel because I want a future.

I had to choose to either die in Syria or make a future. I chose to make a future and they closed the border.

Life in the refugee camp is difficult. Winter is coming and it is very difficult in the tents. Volunteers coming to help is OK but it is not enough for me. We don't want to be here, we want to go to Europe. We don't have money. It is not good food. I have to wait two months for my interview and I can't do anything. I learn some English with Google Translate, and play some football, but we are stuck here.

They have told me I can choose eight countries to go to, but I would go anywhere. I would stay in Greece if I could go to university and have a house, I can make my dream to be a doctor come true. I want to return to Syria. It is my home, my friends, my family, my everything but who knows when I will go back. Maybe I won't see my country again. Maybe I won't see my mother again.

"A refugee is someone who has survived and who can create the future."
Amelia Koluder

Lebanese Salad of Roasted Aubergines and Peppers

These lovely Middle Eastern flavours mixed together make this delicious salad. Serve with fresh bread.

INGREDIENTS

- 6 aubergines
- ½ a red and ½ a green pepper, finely diced and seeds removed
- 4 cloves of garlic, crushed
- 2 lemons, juiced
- 1 bunch of flat leaf parsley, finely chopped
- Handful of coriander, finely chopped
- 4 tbsp extra-virgin olive oil
- 1 tsp ground coriander
- 1 tsp ground cumin

METHOD

Put the aubergines in a very hot oven and roast them for about 45 minutes or until the skins are blackened.

Take them out of the oven and allow to cool.

Scrape out the insides, chop into small chunks and put into a big bowl with the rest of the ingredients. Mix well and serve.

Kaamisha's Story

Kaamisha (35), her two-year-old son Faireh and daughter Azyan (15) are from war-torn Afghanistan and now living in a camp in Lesvos, Greece. After things became just too dangerous in Afghanistan, Kaamisha and her husband decided to make the long and treacherous trek by foot, across snow-covered mountains into Turkey.

In Turkey they gave everything they had to traffickers to take them by boat to Greece. Before they even got to the boat, Iranian border guards started firing at the group. Everyone had to run for their lives but some did not make it. Among those who were killed that day was Kaamisha's husband. Kaamisha had no choice but to continue with the horrific journey, traumatised, lost and alone with her two children. We cannot begin to imagine how she must feel.

Millions of people like Kaamisha are forced to flee their homes because of violence, war and persecution. What will it take for us to become a world where every refugee has a safe place to live and is given the help they need to start to rebuild their broken lives?

> "Refugees only seek a life free from terrorists, war and hunger.
>
> Humanity owes it to them to help them find a safe place to rebuild their lives."

Warm and Spicy Lentil Soup

INGREDIENTS

Serves 4

- 1 carrot, peeled and diced
- 1 onion, diced
- 1 stick of celery, diced
- 4 cloves of garlic, chopped very finely
- 2 tbsp tomato purée
- 2 400g tinned lentils
- 1 400g tinned chopped tomatoes
- 1 litre chicken or vegetable stock
- ½ bunch kale, chopped
- 2 tbsp olive oil

Spices

- 2 tsp of ground cumin
- 2 tsp of ground coriander
- 2 tsp of ground ginger

METHOD

Heat the oil in a large saucepan.

Add the onion, celery and carrot and fry for a few minutes until softened, stirring frequently.

Add the garlic and all the spices and continue to fry for a couple of minutes.

Add the tomato purée and stir well to combine.

Add the stock, tinned tomatoes, lentils and 750ml of water.

Bring this up to a simmer, and leave to cook for about 10 minutes to develop all the delicious flavours.

Add the kale, stir well and allow the kale to wilt. Leave to cook for another few minutes.

The soup is now ready to serve with some lovely crusty bread. Enjoy!

To feel safe and warm
on a cold wet night,
all you need is SOUP.

Comfort food gives you that lovely warm feeling,
whatever the weather.
It makes us feel cared for and carefree.

It can soothe your soul and lift your spirits.

**Baking bread
at the Katsikas
Camp in Greece**

Help a
stranger -
actions speak
louder
than words.

Spinach and Herb Soup

This lip-smacking Lebanese soup has quite an unusual flavour but give it a go; it's healthy and delicious

INGREDIENTS

Serves 4

- 3 tbsp olive oil
- 2 onions, diced
- 4 cloves of garlic, peeled and crushed
- 1 tsp turmeric
- ½ tsp nutmeg
- 2 tsp dried mint
- 250g spinach
- 15g parsley
- 15g coriander
- 600ml vegetable stock
- 60g Greek yoghurt
- 100g feta, crumbled
- Salt and pepper

For serving – some extra feta, mint, parsley and coriander leaves for decoration

METHOD

In a large saucepan, heat the olive oil and then add the onions and garlic. Fry for around 5 minutes until soft.

Add the turmeric and nutmeg and fry for a minute or so before adding the spinach, dried mint, parsley, coriander and stock.

Bring to the boil and then simmer for around 10 minutes.

Blend with a stick blender or liquidise.

Put the yoghurt into a bowl and ladle some of the hot soup into it, then continue to layer the yoghurt and soup so that it doesn't split.

Add the feta and then bring the soup to the boil before serving.

Add the extra herbs and feta to each bowl for decoration, plus a swirl of olive oil.

Quite an unusual flavour, but so healthy and delicious!

Split Pea and Vegetable Soup with Harissa

It's just a handful of humble ingredients, but this vegan soup comes together to make a joyous lunch. Healthy and delicious.

INGREDIENTS

Serves 4

- 2 tbsp olive oil
- 1 red onion, diced
- 4 cloves of garlic, crushed
- 1 red pepper, diced
- 3 sticks of celery, diced
- 2 large or 3 medium carrots, diced
- 1 400g tinned chopped tomatoes
- 500g split peas, soaked overnight if possible (helps the digestion)

- 1 litre vegetable stock
- 2 tsp sea salt
- 2 tsp ground cumin
- 2 tsp ground coriander
- 2 tsp paprika
- 1 tsp chilli flakes
- Salt and pepper, to taste
- 2 tsp harissa paste
- A few parsley or coriander leaves, roughly chopped to garnish

METHOD

Take a very large saucepan and heat the oil before adding the onion. Sauté this until it is soft and then add the garlic, cumin, coriander, paprika and chilli flakes and cook while stirring for another minute or so.

Add the rest of the ingredients and bring to the boil. Cover and turn down to a simmer until the split peas are cooked through. This should take 1 to 1½ hours.

Taste to check the seasoning, then add salt and pepper as necessary.

This is ready to serve so pour into warmed bowls and, if you aren't vegan, you could add a swirl of yoghurt, otherwise just sprinkle the chopped parsley or coriander leaves on the top.

Rana's Story

Rana, a 28-year-old mother from Syria, fled her country after her husband and youngest son were killed in the fighting in her hometown.

She paid traffickers to get her and the rest of her family out of Syria and on to a boat heading for Greece.

Many unsafe makeshift boats were leaving at the same time, and in the chaos, Rana and her daughter Falaq got herded by the traffickers into a different boat to her brother and his wife, who were with her other two children.

The journey was terrifying; Rana witnessed several boats go down and dozens of people drowning in front of her own eyes as they crossed the treacherous seas.

She finally arrived in Lesbos traumatised and exhausted, only to learn that the other boat carrying the rest of her family had not made it.

Persian Marinated Feta

The saltiness of the feta against the warm chillies, tasty onions and sourness of the lemons gives this dish an explosion of flavour.

INGREDIENTS

Serves 4
- 400g feta cheese
- 250ml extra-virgin olive oil
- 1 lemon, zested and juiced
- 3 shallots, finely chopped
- 2 green chillies, deseeded and finely chopped
- 2 red chillies, deseeded and finely chopped
- Large bunch of coriander, finely chopped
- Sea salt, to taste

METHOD

Chop the feta into bite-size chunks and pop into a large tupperware.

Mix the other ingredients together and pour them over the feta.

Leave in the fridge overnight, then when you are ready to serve tip the marinated feta into a serving dish.

Serve with warm fresh bread for dipping.

Every refugee has left a life behind

Tens of thousands of refugees have
been displaced by war, natural
disasters or political catastrophes.
This should remind people that all
the comforts we take for granted can
be taken away in just a moment.

"Show you care. The simplest things mean a lot."

Iranian Chicken Kebabs

These wonderful barbecued kebabs are so moist and succulent. The recipe makes a starter for 4 people, so if you would like to do this as a main course, just double the quantity.

INGREDIENTS

Serves 4

- 2 chicken breasts, cut into strips
- 3 tbsp olive oil
- ½ tsp turmeric
- Pinch of saffron, steeped in a little boiling water
- 1 lemon, juiced
- 2 cloves of garlic, crushed
- 1 red chilli, finely chopped
- 80g tinned chopped tomatoes
- 80g Greek yoghurt

METHOD

Put the chicken pieces into a large bowl with the oil, turmeric, garlic and chilli. Season well with salt and pepper.

Mix well then add the saffron and mix again.

Chill for 1 hour and then add the tomatoes, yoghurt and lemon juice. Leave in the fridge for 6 hours, or overnight.

The marinated chicken can be put straight onto the barbecue or grill, or you can thread them onto skewers, whichever you find easier.

Once they are charred and coloured all over the kebabs are ready to eat. Make sure you don't overcook them though, so they are still soft and succulent in the middle.

Serve with pitta or flatbreads, and some crispy fresh salad and tomatoes.

"No matter what your beliefs or where you live, we are all humans and deserve to be treated with dignity and respect."

Very Tasty Iranian Beef Skewers

INGREDIENTS

Serves 4
- 450g minced beef
- ½ onion, grated
- 2 cloves of garlic, crushed
- 1 tsp baharat spice
- 1 tsp Aleppo pepper (or hot paprika)
- 1 tsp ground allspice
- 25g pine nuts, toasted
- ½ tsp salt
- Handful of flat leaf parsley, very finely chopped

Onion salad goes very well with this: put 1 sliced red onion in a bowl with the juice of 1 lemon, 1 teaspoon of sumac and a pinch of salt. Leave to marinate for at least 30 minutes.

METHOD

Put all the ingredients in a bowl and mix together well. Take a ball of mixture in your hand, form it into a small sausage shape and thread that onto a skewer. You should be able to fit 4 on each skewer.

Grill over a barbecue for about 4 to 5 minutes each side, turning as you go, or do the same under the grill. Once the meat is charred and still juicy they are ready to go.

To serve, it's nice to put some hummus on a serving plate, place the skewers on top and then pile onion salad over the skewers.

Last year the incredible Refugee Community Kitchen in Calais...

SERVED: 2,637,500 MEALS
SUPPORTED: 45,000 PEOPLE
WAS AIDED BY: 17,900 VOLUNTEER HELPERS

Middle Eastern Lamb Koftas with Pistachios

INGREDIENTS

Serves 4

- 500g lean minced lamb
- 1 onion, peeled and grated
- 3 tbsp chopped flat leaf parsley
- 100g pistachios, chopped
- 2 red chillies, deseeded and chopped
- 1½ tsp ground cumin
- 1 tsp ground coriander
- ½ tsp allspice
- Olive oil, for frying
- Salt and pepper

METHOD

Put all the ingredients into a bowl, expect for the olive oil, and mix very well. Make sure the mince is well broken up. Season well with salt and pepper. To test you have the seasoning right, heat a little oil in a frying pan and add a tiny bit of the mixture. Fry and taste this before rolling the koftas, because you can easily add more salt and pepper at this stage if needed.

Take a spoonful of the mince mixture and roll it between your hands to shape into a ball, and then slightly flatten. Repeat with all the mixture.

Once you have made the balls, slide them onto wooden skewers. You shoud get around 4 on each skewer.

Heat up the barbecue or grill, and cook until the koftas are nice and browned on the outside and cooked in the middle. This should take 4 or 5 minutes on each side.

These are lovely served with a yoghurt dressing, rice or flatbreads and a crisp salad.

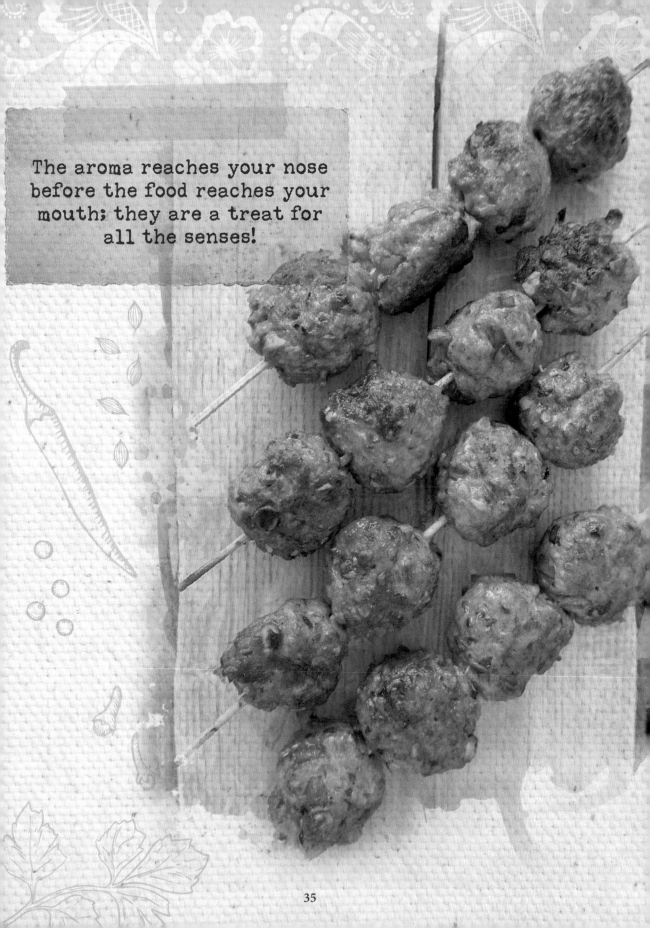

The aroma reaches your nose
before the food reaches your
mouth; they are a treat for
all the senses!

Kuku Sabzi
Persian Herb Frittata

A wonderful Persian take on an omelette, which is full of flavour and colour!

INGREDIENTS

Serves 4

- 100g flat leaf parsley
- 100g coriander
- 20g dill
- 2 tbsp olive oil
- 2 tbsp plain flour
- 2 tsp baking powder
- 1 tsp ground cumin
- ½ tsp ground cinnamon
- 1 tsp ground cardamom
- 1 tsp turmeric
- 2 tsp sea salt
- 4 eggs
- Bunch of spring onions, thinly sliced
- 50g walnuts, chopped
- Freshly ground black pepper

METHOD

Preheat the oven to 180°c and line a 20cm square tin or ovenproof dish with baking paper. Brush all the sides with olive oil.

Put the fresh parsley, coriander, dill and olive oil in a food processor and blend.

Put the flour, baking powder, cumin, cinnamom, cardamom, turmeric and salt in a large bowl and mix well. Add 2 of the eggs and whisk until everything is combined, then add the other eggs and continue whisking until the mixture is smooth.

Add the blended herbs and spring onions to the egg mixture, mixing gently, then stir in the walnuts. Season with black pepper and taste to see if it needs more salt.

Tip the kuku sabzi into the prepared tin and pop into the preheated oven for 25 to 30 minutes until it has set. If you can put a skewer in the centre and it comes out clean, it's ready.

Allow it too cool and then cut into squares. This can be served hot or cold. Some mast o khiar is good with this kuku sabzi.

We are all
entitled
to live
free and
equal

Shakshuka

Gorgeous North African style poached eggs in a spicy tomato sauce.

INGREDIENTS

Serves 4
- 3 tbsp olive oil
- 1 onion, thinly sliced
- 1 red pepper, deseeded and sliced
- 1 red chilli, deseeded and sliced
- 3 cloves of garlic, crushed
- 15g paprika
- 2 tsp ground cumin
- 400g tinned chopped tomatoes
- Salt and pepper, to taste
- Handful of fresh coriander
- 6 eggs

METHOD

Heat the olive oil in a large deep frying pan. Add the onion, red pepper and chilli in one layer, spread out so everything is in contact with the bottom of the pan.

Fry these without moving them for 5 or 6 minutes until they are very browned on the bottom, soft and a little bit charred.

Add the garlic, paprika and cumin to the pan then cook for another minute. Add the tomatoes and stir everything together.

Reduce the heat and simmer for 10 minutes, then add the salt and pepper to taste.

Sprinkle in half the coriander, and now add the eggs. Make a well using a large spoon, near the edge of the pan, and crack an egg into it. Repeat with each of the eggs. Make sure the yolks are exposed. Sprinkle a little salt on each egg.

Cover the pan and reduce the heat to low and then cook until the white of the eggs are firm but the yolks are runny. This should take about 8 minutes.

Sprinkle the rest of the coriander over the top, then take the pan over to the table and serve!

Courgette, Feta and Herb Fritters

Little bits of loveliness that melt in your mouth, adapted from an Afghan recipe.

INGREDIENTS

Serves 4

- 3 tbsp flour
- 3 eggs
- 2 courgettes
- 1 red onion, cut in half and then into thin half moon slices
- 200g feta cheese, crumbled
- 2 green chillies, finely chopped
- ½ bunch of flat leaf parsley, finely chopped
- Bunch of mint, finely chopped
- Splash of olive oil

METHOD

Put the flour and eggs into a bowl and beat them together until smooth.

Coarsely grate the courgettes into a tea towel, then use it to squeeze out all the liquid.

Add the grated courgette and the rest of the dry ingredients to the flour and eggs. Stir well to create a smooth mixture.

Heat a little bit of olive oil in a frying pan and then add 3 to 4 spoonfuls of the mixture, leaving space between for the fritters to expand. 1 spoonful makes 1 fritter.

Fry over a medium heat for 2 to 3 minutes on each side, pressing them firmly as they cook, and flip them over when they are lightly browned.

Cook in batches, adding a little extra oil with each batch.

As you finish a batch keep them warm under foil until serving.

Serve immediately.
The broad bean salad works brilliantly with them.
Really lovely summer's lunch.

Exercise your smile muscles
Volunteer for refugee support
It will change your life.

"Smile more often, laugh a bit louder,
treat others with dignity, show more
compassion, be less judgmental, give more
love and less hate. We are all humans."

Grilled Aubergine with Harissa and Yoghurt

These are so simple to make, but an absolute gastronomic delight.

INGREDIENTS

Serves 4
- 2 aubergines
- 3 tbsp harissa
- 3 tbsp olive oil
- 1 tsp sea salt

For the yoghurt sauce
- 150ml yoghurt
- 1 lime, juiced
- 1 clove of garlic, crushed
- 3 tbsp finely chopped fresh coriander

METHOD

Cut the aubergine into thin rounds about ½cm thick.

Mix the harissa, olive oil and salt together to make a paste and brush it over both sides of the aubergine slices.

Grill the slices on a hot barbecue, turning as they cook, until charred and tender. This should take around 10 minutes.

Mix the ingredients for the yoghurt sauce together.

Once the aubergines are cooked, put them on a large plate, drizzle the yoghurt sauce over and serve.

Lovely with any grilled meats or other vegetables

> "For days when warmth is the greatest need of the human heart, the most important emotions come from the kitchen. The aromas and familiarity of comfort food cannot be beaten."

Easy and so tasty

Grilled Courgettes

Melt in your mouth
courgettes with a touch
of spice. Perfect with
all barbecues.

INGREDIENTS

Serves 4
- 4 courgettes
- 2 tbsp olive oil
- 2 tbsp za'atar spice
- 2 tsp salt
- 4 cloves of garlic, crushed

METHOD

Slice the courgettes on the diagonal,
about ½cm thick, and place into
large bowl. Add the olive oil and toss
through with your hands, then add
the za'atar, garlic and salt. Distribute
everything evenly by tossing the
mixture with your hands. Put the
courgette slices on the hot barbecue
or griddle pan and cook through until
there are good grill marks and then
turn over to cook the other side.

"Life becomes more meaningful if we are able to find ways to help others through their darkest moments."

KATISKAS RESIDENT MOHAMMAD NABEEL-
HIS EXPERIENCE IS SADLY ALL TOO FAMILIAR

"When it comes to human dignity we cannot make any compromise."
Angela Merkel

Mohammad's Story

For all the thousands of Syrians you have provided with refuge, thank you.

I grew up in a Palestinian refugee camp in Syria, which was bombed. Missiles and mortar killed my friends and burnt my home.

I never wanted to leave Syria, but I had no choice. I was arrested and tortured by the Regime for six months. It felt like 60 years. They hung me for three hours each day in a one by one metre cell. I shared a cell with two other men; we had to sleep standing up because there wasn't enough space. I thought I was dead. They accused me of being a rebel, but I had never fought in my life.

My shoulders cracked. I can't even carry my child. When you enter interrogation, you are totally naked. People are dying and screaming in front of you. They hit me with electricity cables. But the most difficult part is the hanging. I was blindfolded and often lost consciousness.

When I finally came out of prison, I went home. But what I saw was incomprehensible. At each side of my town, militia were fighting each other with missiles. My wife was shot. Food was not available, and used as a weapon of war. My wife - Rania - was pregnant, but we lost our baby.

I had no choice but to leave. I carried my son and my wife – who could barely walk because the bullet was still in her knee - the best I could. We walked to Turkey, and eventually arrived in Greece. They call it 'The Journey of Death.'

We had reached safety, but we were unprepared for what was to come.

After walking for two days, we were given a tent filled with rain. I had to use my only clothes to mop up the dirt. My son cried because it was so cold. Rats played inside the tent. My child didn't understand why we had to leave. He developed a serious fever, but there was no ambulance and I had no money to transport him to the hospital. I walked for miles, and carried him on my cracked shoulders. Would we have been better off in Syria?

My family now live in a container in a field. I am an engineer, and my wife is a successful wedding photographer, but we are not allowed to work. I don't want to live on handouts, but we have no choice. We are at the mercy of government policies, and must wait until December 2019 for our next interview to claim asylum.

I feel so much shame, that I can't provide for my wife and son. I am humiliated. We are stuck, a number in a system.

Even if I get residency in Greece, I have no passport, so I can't visit my sister in Turkey or my mother who is still trapped in Syria. There is also no work here. I don't want anything from this life, I am not asking for money, housing or clothes. All I want is to secure a dignified life for my wife and son. I want to sweat, and work for their future. We are strong, we have survived pain only Syrians can understand. But I need a new kind of strength: hope.

I miss my family. I haven't seen them in three years. My brother is still imprisoned by the Regime, I pray he is alive. Why is it my sin, that I was born in Syria? Born as a Palestinian with no rights, no identity?

In the name of my family, I appeal to anyone who will listen. Is it not our right to sleep on a bed? Buy our own food? Protect our children from falling bullets?

Who knows. I sit in my container, waiting…and waiting. Trapped. Helpless.

It is not our right to live too?

Middle Eastern Courgettes
Stuffed with Fragrant Rice

Courgettes are so popular in the Middle East and such a versatile ingredient. This recipe for stuffing them with rice and lots of different textures and flavours makes a really aromatic and tasty meal.

INGREDIENTS

Serves 4

- 1 tbsp olive oil
- 1 onion, finely chopped
- 100g rice
- 2 tsp currants
- 1 tbsp pine nuts
- 2 tbsp flat leaf parsley
- ½ tsp of each of these spices:
- Allspice
- Cinnamon
- Ground clove
- Dried mint
- 1 lemon, juiced
- 3 courgettes
- 200ml boiling water
- 1 tbsp sugar
- Salt and pepper

METHOD

Heat the oil in a frying pan, add the onion and fry until softened.

Add the rice, currants, pine nuts, parsley, all the spices and half the lemon juice. Fry the mixture slowly for 5 minutes.

Halve the courgettes length ways and scoop out the seeds.

Take a large flat frying pan and sit the courgettes on the base, cut side up. Fill the boats with the stuffing.

Pour the boiling water into the frying pan (the liquid should come half way up the courgette) then add the remaining lemon juice, sprinkle on the sugar and add some salt and pepper.

Cover the pan and simmer for 30 to 40 minutes, basting the stuffing occasionally with the juices.

The stuffed courgettes are ready when the rice is just al dente. The juices should have almost all evaporated (if at any stage in the cooking the pan goes dry add a little extra water).

Sprinkle with some more chopped parsley and serve.

Turkish Menemen Scrambled Eggs

INGREDIENTS

Serves 4

- 2 long green or red peppers
- 2 large tomatoes, peeled
- 4 tbsp olive oil
- 4 large eggs, whisked very gently
- Pinch of salt and pepper
- Pinch of red chilli flakes
- Pinch of dried thyme

METHOD

Deseed and chop the peppers very finely, then dice the tomatoes.

Heat the olive oil in a heavy-bottomed frying pan and then add the peppers. Fry for a few minutes, add the tomatoes and cook over medium heat for about 5 minutes until nearly all the moisture has evaporated.

Add the eggs and fold them into the tomato mixture.

Stir the mixture for a few minutes until the eggs are softly cooked.

Remove from the heat and add the salt and black pepper, chilli flakes, and thyme.

Serve straight from the pan with some lovely fresh bread for dipping.

Great way to start the day!

"When we are children we only know what is happening now.

We have no thoughts or plans for the future, no regrets about the past.

We are able to immerse ourselves and really be in the moment.

Why then as adults do we lose the ability to live life this way?"

Whole Middle Eastern Shawarma Cauliflower
with Tahini Sauce

One of London's most influential restaurants specialising in Middle Eastern and North African cuisine have kindly allowed us to include one of their signature dish recipes.

If you want to see how the experts do it, pop into **Berber & Q** and give it a try.

INGREDIENTS

Serves 4
- 1 cauliflower

For the spiced butter
- 40g unsalted butter, softened to room temperature
- 1 lemon, juiced
- 1 clove of garlic, crushed
- 2 tbsp chopped coriander
- 1 tbsp ground cinnamon
- 1 tbsp sumac
- 2 tsp ground cumin
- ½ tsp ground allspice
- Pinch of ground cardamom

For the tahini sauce
- 100g tahini
- 1 tbsp lemon juice
- 1 clove of garlic, crushed
- 1 tbsp pomegranate molasses, thined down with a little water
- 100ml iced water

For the garnish
- 2 tbsp pomegranate seeds
- 1 tbsp pine nuts, toasted
- 1 green chilli, sliced
- 1 tbsp chopped flat leaf parsley
- Drizzle of olive oil

METHOD

Firstly make the spiced butter that gives all the wonderful flavour to the cauliflower.

Put all the ingredients for the butter into a processor and blend until they are combined.

Next, make the tahini sauce. Either blitz the ingredients in a food processor or whisk by hand, gradually adding the iced water as a trickle. The thickness of the sauce should be similar to custard.

Preheat the oven to its hottest setting.

Meanwhile, trim the big outer leaves off the cauliflower, leaving the smaller ones on.

Fill a huge saucepan with salted water and bring it to the boil, then carefully lower the whole cauliflower in, making sure the water covers it completely. Then bring it back up to a rolling boil and leave the cauliflower in there for about 6 to 8 minutes until it is al dente. Try not to overcook it as it shouldn't be too soft.

Take it out and put it on a cooling rack over a roasting tin.

Spread the spiced butter all over the cauliflower, leaving about 2 tablespoons to use later. Try to get between the cracks in the florets to get as much coverage as possible.

Pop the cauliflower into the oven on the cooling rack in the roasting tin, and roast in the oven for 5 to 7 minutes until it is blackened, but not burnt, all over.

Spread the remaining butter over the cauliflower then put it on the barbecue floret side down to grill for few minutes, adding extra flavour.

Now it is ready to dress, so put the cauliflower on a serving plate and pour over the tahini sauce, then sprinkle on all the garnishes. Finish with a drizzle of olive oil.

Eat straight away – sooo good!

Broad Bean Salad
Middle Eastern Style

Nothing beats the fresh taste of a beautiful
broad bean salad. We love this one!

INGREDIENTS

Serves 4
- 500g frozen broad beans,
  cooked and podded
- 2 tomatoes, chopped
- 1 small red onion, diced
- ½ cucumber, diced
- 2 cloves of garlic, crushed
- ½ bunch of fresh parsley
- 1 lemon, juiced
- 3 tbsp olive oil
- 1 tsp ground cumin
- Salt and black pepper, to taste

METHOD

Combine the broad beans,
tomatoes, onion and cucumber
in a bowl. Add the garlic, parsley,
lemon juice and olive oil. Mix well
and then stir in the cumin, salt and
pepper to taste.

The salad is ready to serve straight
away, or can be kept in the fridge for
up to 6 hours.

It goes well with barbecues or
grills because the flavours are so
fresh and summery.

"Treat us with respect
and dignity. If we have
that we can survive on
bread and water."

Middle Eastern Green Salad

with Dukkah Olive Oil

This is a lovely mixture of green leaves, nuts and spices.

fresh and tasty!

INGREDIENTS

Serves 4

- 1 bag of mixed green leaves such as spinach, watercress and kale
- 1 baby gem lettuce, root removed then quartered and sliced
- ½ medium red onion
- ½ cucumber, sliced into ½ cm slices
- 2 tbsp pomegranate seeds
- 2 tbsp pine nuts, toasted
- 2 tbsp coarsely chopped toasted hazelnuts
- 20 mint leaves, finely chopped plus a few extra for garnish
- 1 tbsp lemon juice
- 3 tbsp extra-virgin olive oil
- Salt and pepper, to taste
- 4 tbsp dukkah
- Pinch of sumac

METHOD

Arrange the salad leaves in a large bowl, and then sprinkle on the onion, cucumber, pomegranate seeds, nuts and mint leaves.

Mix the lemon juice and olive oil together, add the salt and pepper, then drizzle onto the salad and give it a good toss so everything is covered with the dressing. Use your hands if you can.

Sprinkle the dukkah on the top and finish off with a small pinch of sumac.

Ready to go!

"FOR A START,
PEOPLE WHO HAVE TRAVELLED
FOR SO MANY MILES
THROUGH SUCH HORRIFIC
CONDITIONS IN ORDER TO
FIND WORK CANNOT
ACCURATELY BE PORTRAYED
AS LAZY BENEFIT SCROUNGERS."

Patrick Kingsley

Tabbouleh

This Middle Eastern salad is so versatile, either as a starter or part of a main course.

INGREDIENTS

Serves 4

- 100g bulgur wheat
- 4 plum tomatoes (or 12 small ones)
- 6 spring onions
- Large bunch of flat leaf parsley, leaves picked
- ½ bunch of mint, leaves picked
- ¼ tsp allspice
- ¼ tsp cinnamon
- 1 lemon, juiced
- 3 tbsp extra-virgin olive oil
- 3 tbsp pomegranate seeds

METHOD

Cook the bulgar wheat according to the instructions on the packet, then rinse with cold water and leave to drain.

Finely chop the tomatoes, spring onions, parsley and mint leaves and then add to a large bowl with the bulgar wheat.

Mix the spices together and then add to the bulgar wheat, then add the lemon juice and olive oil.

Sprinkle on the pomegranate seeds and serve.

58

"Refugees have not just escaped a place. They have escaped a thousand memories."

"We may have different religions, different languages, different coloured skin, but we all belong to one human race."

Kofi Annan

Tomato and Pomegranate Salad

This bright side dish looks lovely
and is so full of flavour.

INGREDIENTS

Serves 4

- 2 cloves of garlic, crushed
- ½ tsp allspice
- 2 tsp white wine vinegar
- 1 tbsp pomegranate molasses
- 60ml olive oil
- Salt and black pepper, to taste
- 800g assorted tomatoes (try to get a mix
  of cherry and large tomatoes, yellow and
  plum to give a good range of size and
  colour) chopped into ½cm dice
- 1 small red onion, finely diced
- 1 pomegranate, seeds removed
- Few sprigs of fresh oregano

METHOD

Whisk the garlic, allspice, vinegar,
pomegranate molasses, olive oil and
about ½ a teaspoon of salt together
in a large bowl.

Add the tomatoes and onion
then gently turn over to combine
everything. You can use your hands
for this.

Tip the salad onto a serving platter
and sprinkle the pomegranate seeds
on the top and then decorate with
the oregano.

Serve with any grilled meats or veggies

Cultivate kindness

"Refugees and migrants are not pawns
on a chess board of humanity."
Pope Francis

They are children,
women and men
who have been forced to flee
their homelands

and deserve to be treated with
compassion and humanity.

Musham's Story

Musham was selling potatoes when a Russian air-strike bombed the Aleppo market in Syria where he was working. 57 people died and 75 were wounded, including many of his friends, in what he calls a massacre.

He lost his leg.

'My wife ran out of the house barefoot with our two babies to find me,' he recalls. They fled Aleppo, a key battleground of the civil war. Many neighbourhoods have been completed destroyed and most of the city lies in rubble.

Musham's son is four years old, and hasn't spoken for over six months. He refuses to talk, or eat. His father mimics a plane exploding: 'he is scared of the bombs.'

Musham and his family are in Katiskas camp in Greece, where they are stuck. Their future remains uncertain.

"We can't simply rely on politicians and world leaders to bring justice and dignity to the refugee crisis. It's the duty of humanity to help these people. This includes you and I."

Asparagus, broad bean and garlic salad

This mouthwatering Middle Eastern style salad is so fresh and tasty. Enjoy as part of mezze starters or a fab side dish to any grill.

Irresistible!

INGREDIENTS

Serves 4
- 3 tbsp extra-virgin olive oil
- 4 spring onions, thinly sliced
- 5 cloves of garlic, crushed
- 2 bunches of fresh asparagus (the small thinner kind is best)
- 500g broad beans, shelled
- 1 tbsp lemon juice
- 1 lemon, zested
- Salt and pepper, to taste

METHOD

Heat the oil in a large frying pan, then add the spring onions and garlic and fry gently for a few minutes.

Chop the asparagus into bite-size pieces, add to the pan and fry for a few minutes until is it just tender before adding the broad beans. Continue to cook for a few minutes and then add the lemon juice and zest.

Taste the salad, then add salt and pepper as necessary.

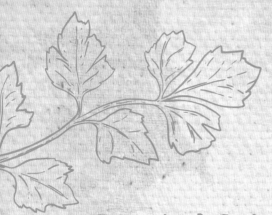

Roasted Spiced Butternut Squash

Adding these spices to the squash makes it sing!

INGREDIENTS

Serves 4

- 1 butternut squash
- 3 tbsp baharat spice mix
- 3 tbsp olive oil
- Sea salt
- 100g Greek yoghurt
- ½ bunch of mint
- 1 tsp sumac
- 2 tsp ground coriander
- 1 tbsp olive oil
- 1 lemon, juiced and zested
- 2 red chillies, finely sliced
- 2 tsp nigella seeds
- Handful of flat leaf parsley, finely chopped

METHOD

Preheat the oven to 220°c and line a baking tray with foil or baking paper.

Peel the squash and then cut down the middle and scoop out the seeds.

Cut both halves horizontally at the bulge so you have 4 pieces. Cut these pieces again so you have 8 pieces.

You can cut each piece into 2 or 3 depending on the size but try to end up with quite evenly sized pieces.

Put the baharat spice in a bowl with the olive oil and mix to make a paste, then add the squash and rub the paste all over to make sure every piece is covered.

Tip the squash onto the baking sheet and spread out, then season it with sea salt.

Roast in the preheated oven for around 40 minutes until the squash is cooked through and nicely browned. Tip onto a serving dish.

Mix the yoghurt, mint, sumac, coriander, olive oil, lemon zest and juice together. Season with salt and pepper and then put spoonfuls of the yoghurt mix in dollops on top of the squash. Sprinkle on the chillies, nigella seeds and parsley.

So good!

"Look at the world with
an open heart."

The world must not turn away from the Rohingya crisis

Over 720,000 Rohingya children, women and men have been forced to flee to Bangladesh, escaping violence in Myanmar since August 2017.

The majority walked for days through jungles and mountains, or braved dangerous sea voyages across the Bay of Bengal, carrying what little they could bring from home. They arrive exhausted, hungry and sick, in need of international protection and humanitarian assistance.

Rohingya families have already endured so much suffering. We cannot abandon them now.

'Kinye is only 12 but has already endured traumas many of us can only begin to imagine. She watched as her childhood home was burnt down. As she tried to escape with her family her two brothers were killed in front of her, one set alight and one thrown into the river.'

More than 911,000 people fled violence in Myannar and are now living in refugee camps in Bangladesh (UNICEF, April 2019) surviving in extremely basic conditions. Of these an estimated 7700 are orphans.

What makes life more bearable for children living in refugee camps is a safe space to recover from the trauma they have endured and to just be children.

Fattoush Salad with Avocado

This salad can be served on its own, but the dressing really makes it quite special. It's a lovely side dish for any summer meal.

INGREDIENTS

Serves 4

- 2 bags of mixed salad leaves
- 1 baby gem lettuce
- 8 sweet baby tomatoes, halved
- 6 radishes, cut in half and sliced very thinly
- 1 avocado, stoned and sliced
- 2 baby cucumbers, halved lengthwise and then cut into half moons
- 2-3 tbsp olive oil
- 2 pitta breads, cut into strips

Dressing

- 4 tbsp extra-virgin olive oil
- 1 shallot, very finely chopped
- 1 tbsp runny honey
- 2 tsp pomegranate molasses
- 2 tbsp red wine vinegar

METHOD

Put all the dressing ingredients into a jam jar and shake to mix.

On your large serving plate or dish, arrange the green leaves and baby gem prettily and then sprinkle on the tomatoes, radishes, avocado and cucumber.

Heat the olive oil in a frying pan then fry the pitta bread in batches until lovely and crisp.

Sprinkle these on the top of the salad and then pour over the dressing. Take to the table with serving spoons and toss it all together, then tuck in.

"Sharing food
is the most
basic form
of comfort.

Home-cooked food
not only warms
you but
is a constant
reminder
of your
mother's kitchen."

African Cabbage Salad

It is nice to have both red and green cabbage as it looks great, but don't worry if you only have one colour; it tastes just as good.

INGREDIENTS

Serves 4

For the salad

- 3 spring onions
- 4 sprigs of mint, leaves picked
- 4 sprigs of parsley, leaves picked
- ½ small green cabbage and ½ small red cabbage or 1 of either, cored, shredded and finely chopped
- 2 carrots, peeled and grated
- 3 large tomatoes, finely diced

For the dressing

- 120ml extra-virgin olive oil
- 2 lemons, juiced
- Sea salt
- Freshly ground black pepper

METHOD

Place the spring onions, mint and parsley in a food processor and chop finely. Mix this with all the other salad ingredients.

Whisk the dressing ingredients together, then drizzle over the salad. Stir everything together, taste and adjust the seasoning, then serve!

Crunchy, colourful and bursting with flavour!

Roasted Spiced Carrots with Yoghurt Topping

An exotic Iraqi side dish to enhance any table.

INGREDIENTS

- 600g carrots, peeled, topped and tailed
- 3 cloves of garlic, crushed
- Thumb-sized piece of root ginger, sliced
- 1 tsp ground cumin
- 1 tsp black mustard seeds
- 1 tsp ground coriander
- ½ tsp ground cinnamon
- ½ tsp allspice
- ½ tsp ground ginger

- ½ tsp dried chilli flakes
- 1 lemon, juiced
- 3 tbsp olive oil
- Sea salt and fresh black pepper, for seasoning

For the yoghurt topping
- 150g Greek yogurt
- ½ bunch fresh coriander
- ½ bunch fresh dill
- 1 lemon, juiced

METHOD

Preheat the oven to 180°c. Chop the carrots in half lengthways, and then do the same again with each half so you have four pieces. Put the carrots and all the other ingredients, except those for the topping, into a bowl and mix well.

Tip them onto a baking tray and pop in the preheated oven for 30 to 40 minutes until they are cooked through and nicely charred.

Put the ingredients for the topping into a food processor, add a couple of spoonfuls of water and blend to create a smooth sauce.

When the carrots are ready, take them out of the oven and discard the ginger.

Put the carrots onto a serving dish and drizzle over the yoghurt sauce, then it's ready for the table.

"How can the world stand by and watch as thousands of innocent humans are driven from their homes and forced to risk their lives on the open seas, praying they can find a new life in peace and safety?"

Khan Ali's Story

**Now living in
Katsikas camp
in Greece.**

My name is Khan Ali. There are a lot
of people on camp from many different
countries, and this can cause friction on
a camp this big. They come because of
many reasons, but we are all in the same
position here.

Last year I decided to make a farm around my container, but I had to change container after my wife left for Germany so lost my little garden.

My job back in Afghanistan was working in an office. But I love to garden.

When I saw that Refugee Support was creating a community garden I loved the idea and asked if I could have an allotment.

We started to plant the seeds in March in each of the allotments. Peas, chard, courgettes. I would go and care for the garden every day.

I then asked if I could have a larger allotment right along the fence. My friend and I started to dig, and now we have tomatoes, onions and okra. It's growing beautifully.

I would like to thank Refugee Support, especially Dan and John.

The shop means a lot to everyone on camp. It's not just about the food though. There is a lot happening there, such as women's classes, children's activities, and the cinema.

It's all happening because of kind people from Refugee Support. Thank you.

Mejadra

Arabic rice and lentils with crispy onions

Something magical happens when you mix the rice and lentils together with these spices and top with crispy onions. There are no bells and whistles with this dish but it is simply irresistible.

INGREDIENTS

Serves 4
- 250g green or brown lentils
- 4 onions (about 700g)
- 100ml sunflower oil
- 1 tbsp cumin seeds
- 200g basmati rice
- 2 tsp ground coriander
- 1½ tsp allspice
- 1½ tsp ground turmeric
- 1½ tsp ground cinnamon
- Salt and black pepper
- 350ml water

METHOD

Put the lentils in a saucepan and cover with cold water, then bring to the boil and cook for about 15 minutes until they have softened. Drain and set aside.

Peel and very thinly slice the onions into half moons. Heat the oil in a large heavy-bottomed pan (you will be using this to cook the rice later) and once it is hot add the onions. Fry, stirring occasionally, for about 7 minutes until they are golden brown and crispy.

Remove the onions with a slotted spoon and leave to drain on a plate or in a colander lined with kitchen paper.

Put the pan back on the heat, add the cumin seeds and toast them for a minute or so before adding the rice, all the spices and about ½ a teaspoon of sea salt and plenty of black pepper.

"Offer your hand
to a stranger from
another race, culture
or background. Not just
because they are nice,
but because you
are nice."

Add the lentils to the rice mixture and stir well before adding the water.

Give everything another stir to make sure it is all mixed, bring to the boil, cover with a lid and then turn the heat down as low as you can and cook for 20 minutes.

Take the pan off the heat, and leave it to sit for 10 minutes with the lid on.

Add half of the fried onions to the rice, and then put the rice and lentil mixture onto a serving platter and scatter the rest of the onions on top.

"Refugees are not like you and me,
they are you and me." Richard Flanagan

Ethiopian Chicken Stew Doro Wot

This recipe is from the lovely Belay who we met in Katsikas Camp. He always had a smile on his face and was so happy to spend time with us. When we asked him for his favourite recipe from home, his face lit up as he told us that this was the best dish you could eat!

INGREDIENTS

Serves 4

- 6 tbsp oil (any vegetable oil is fine)
- 8 chicken thighs
- 2 onions, sliced into thin half moons
- 3 cloves of garlic, crushed
- 2½cm of ginger, peeled and grated
- 1 tbsp tomato paste
- Salt and pepper, to taste
- 3 tsp paprika
- 4 hard boiled eggs, shell removed (optional but definitely authentic)
- 1 lemon, juiced

The berbere spice is what makes this taste so delicious and different. It's not easy to get hold of, so I made my own and have kept it in a jar ready to use on any grilled meats as a rub.

For the berbere spice

- 60g dried chillies (Mexican if possible)
- 30g paprika
- 1 tbsp cayenne pepper
- 1 tsp onion power
- 1 tsp ground ginger
- 1 tsp ground cumin
- 1 tsp ground coriander
- 1 tsp ground cardamom
- 1 tsp ground fenugreek
- ½ tsp ground cinnamon
- 1 tsp ground allspice
- ½ tsp ground cloves

**Lovely with rice and some
fresh green vegetables**

METHOD

Heat 2 tablespoons of the oil in
large casserole.

Fry the chicken pieces on both sides
until they are lovely and brown.

Remove from the pan and set aside
on a plate.

Add some more of the oil to the pan
and fry the onions until they are a deep
brown colour, then add a little more oil
and the berbere spice, garlic and ginger.

Stir fry for another 2 to 3 minutes,
before adding the chicken pieces
back in along with the tomato paste,
paprika, some salt and pepper and 2 cups
of water. Leave to cook slowly for
30 minutes.

Add the eggs if using, and make
sure they are immersed in the sauce,
then add the lemon juice.

Continue cooking for another 10
minutes or more and then serve.

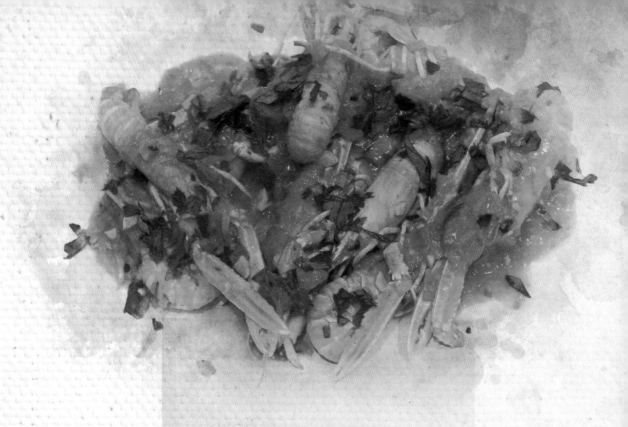

Prawns Alla Busara

Savour the magical flavour
of these scrumptious
African prawns!

INGREDIENTS

- 100ml olive oil
- 24 large shell-on prawns or langoustines
- 3 shallots, finely chopped
- 3 cloves of garlic, finely chopped
- 2 large tomatoes, chopped
- 1 tbsp tomato paste
- ½ tsp saffron strands, dissolved in hot water
- Pinch of chilli flakes
- 1 tsp salt and black pepper
- 350ml fish stock (a mild flavour is best)
- 2 tbsp breadcrumbs
- Handful of chopped flat leaf parsley

METHOD

Put about 30ml of the olive oil in a deep sided frying pan over a high heat. Once hot, add the prawns. Fry the prawns until the shells are nice and crispy; keep turning them. Once they are browned all over take them out and put them to one side.

Add the rest of the olive oil to the pan and then add the shallots and garlic.

Fry for a couple of minutes and then add the chopped tomatoes and tomato paste, saffron in hot water, chilli flakes and ½ a teaspoon of salt, stirring continuously.

After a couple of minutes add the stock and then reduce the heat. Leave to simmer and reduce for about 20 minutes.

Add the prawns to the sauce and coat them well. Leave them to cook in the sauce for 5 minutes or so, then add the breadcrumbs to thicken the sauce.

Add more salt and black pepper to taste, then sprinkle over the parsley and serve.

Marwan Mahmood's Story

We met Marwan and heard his story when we were volunteering in Cyprus, where he is now a refugee.

My name is Marwan Mahmood. I am 33 and was born and raised in Gaza. Since I was a young boy in Gaza all I ever wanted was to live in peace and to help bring an end to the violence and killing between the Palestinian and Israeli people. I am a committed peace activist and have participated in many events that have allowed me to befriend many like-minded Israeli people, who share my views and desires and are happy to work together and to share positive ideas and actions.

When Hamas learned about my activities and my open friendship with the Israeli people I got arrested several times and became a target which resulted in me getting badly injured and then being treated at an Israeli hospital.

They did not want the outside world to know that there are many people here who want peace, and want to live as friends with our neighbours.

My ID papers got confiscated after my treatment in hospital and I realised that it was not safe for me to return to my family in Gaza.

Frightened for my safety, I realised I had to seek asylum in Europe.

With help from friends I found a way to get to Turkey via Jordan, but due to close relations between Turkey and Hamas I was still not safe, and the Turkish embassy blocked my visa into Europe. From Turkey I had to borrow funds to get to the Greek side of Cyprus.

For the first time in years I feel safe here in Cyprus, and in general the Cypriot people are friendly and welcoming to the many refugees that are seeking refuge here.

Daily life is tough, however, as I am not allowed to work and I could take as long as 18 months to go through the asylum procedure to hopefully gain full refugee status. We have nowhere to live and the social welfare allowance is not even enough to cover the minimum requirement for food and daily life.

I am determined to continue my vital peace work in the future but for now I will give back to the people of Cyprus by volunteering for the local Red Cross who are very kind and helpful to other refugees.

Cauliflower and Chickpea Tagine

Really tasty vegan dish, with the lovely warming flavour of harissa. This truly one pot recipe is a simple dish to make midweek, on your own or with friends.

INGREDIENTS

Serves 4

- 2 tbsp olive oil
- 1 onion, chopped
- 2 cloves of garlic, crushed
- 2 tsp coriander seeds, toasted ground (you can use ground coriander if preferred but the freshly ground seeds have more flavour)
- 1 cauliflower, trimmed and cut into florets
- 400g tinned chickpeas
- 400g tinned chopped tomatoes
- 1 tsp sugar
- 2 tsp harissa
- ½ lemon, juiced
- Small bunch of fresh coriander, finely chopped

Lovely served with rice.

METHOD

Take a heavy saucepan or tagine and heat the oil before adding the chopped onion. Fry for a few minutes until the onion is soft, then add the garlic and coriander seeds. Fry for a few minutes before adding the cauliflower and chickpeas.

Stir the mixture for a minute or so and then add the tomatoes, sugar and enough water to just cover the cauliflower.

Bring to the boil and then pop on the lid, reduce the heat and simmer for around 15 to 20 minutes until the cauliflower is tender.

Remove the lid and add the harissa, lemon juice and half of the chopped fresh coriander. Cook for another 5 minutes.

Sprinkle over the rest of the coriander and then this one pot meal is ready to serve!

Kuwaiti Fish Stew with Dried Limes

Refugee Support Let's Eat Event

INGREDIENTS

- 2 tsp ground cumin
- 2 tsp ground black pepper
- 2 tsp ground cardamom
- 2 tsp ground turmeric
- 2 tsp salt
- 2 tbsp plain flour
- 3 tbsp vegetable oil
- 2 onions, finely chopped
- 3 large tomatoes
- 3 tbsp tomato paste
- 2 dried limes, pieced 4 or 5 times each with a skewer
- 1 large green chilli, finely chopped
- 3 cloves of garlic, crushed
- 4 monkfish fillets
- 500ml water
- Large bunch of fresh coriander, leaves chopped
- Large bunch of dill leaves, chopped

Really tasty!

METHOD

Mix all the spices and salt together, and then combine with the flour.

Heat the 2 tablespoons of oil in a large frying pan and fry the onions. Once they are soft and translucent, add the tomatoes, tomato paste, pierced dried limes, chilli, garlic and 2 teaspoons of the spice mixture.

Pat the fish fillets dry and then coat them in the spiced flour.

In a separate frying pan, heat the rest of the oil and fry the fish for 1 minute on each side.

Then add the fish to the stew mixture along with the water. Make sure it is covered, adding more water if necessary.

Add half of the coriander and dill, then simmer gently for 10 to 15 minutes until the fish flakes easily with a fork.

Sprinkle over the rest of the dill and coriander and the stew is ready to serve.

This is particularly good with rice and a green vegetable like spinach or chard.

"Sharing food is the best way of bringing people together, and building friendships."

Chicken Shawarma

INGREDIENTS

Serves 4

- 800g chicken thighs, skinless and boneless
- 2 tbsp ground cumin
- 2 tbsp ground coriander
- 4 cloves of garlic, crushed
- 2 tsp salt
- 3 tbsp olive oil
- ¼ tsp cayenne
- 2 tsp tumeric
- ½ tsp ground black pepper
- ½ tsp ground ginger
- 1tsp allspice

Delicious

METHOD

Place all the ingredients except the chicken in a bowl and mix well to make a paste.

Rub this all over the chicken and leave to marinate in the fridge for 30 minutes or overnight if possible.

Grill or barbecue the chicken until it is lovely and crisp on the outside and cooked through on the inside.

A favourite with my family

Roast Lamb Koftas

With Beans and Roasted Couscous

INGREDIENTS

Serves 4

- 300g couscous or bulgar wheat
- 1 tsp cumin seeds
- 1 tsp coriander seeds
- 2 tsp sumac (or substitue for 1 tbsp lemon)
- 600g mince
- 1 small onion, grated
- 3 cloves of garlic, crushed
- ½ bunch of mint, chopped
- 1 tbsp olive oil, plus extra for drizzling
- 200g green beans, cut into bite-size pieces
- 2 tbsp runny honey
- 1 lemon, zested and juiced
- 280ml thick Greek yoghurt

> "It is the obligation of every person born in a safer room to open the door when someone in danger knocks."
>
> Dina Nayeri, author of The Ungrateful Refugee

METHOD

Preheat the oven to 200°c.

Put the couscous into a heatproof roasting pot that you will be using for the dish and add 375ml of hot water. Cover and leave for 5 minutes, until the water has been absorbed.

Crush the cumin and coriander seeds with a pestle and mortar and then add half of the sumac (or lemon juice).

Add the mince, onion, garlic, mint and olive oil to the spice mix. Combine well.

Roll the kofta mixture into 16 walnut-sized balls.

Place the balls on top of the couscous along with the beans, then drizzle with honey and olive oil.

Pop the dish into the oven for 30 minutes or until the meatballs are browned and cooked through.

Add the lemon zest and juice to the yoghurt and drizzle that over the dish with the remaining sumac.

Scatter a few mint leaves over the top and serve.

Warming Sweet Potato, Carrot, Lentil and Spinach Vegan Curry

INGREDIENTS

Serves 4

- 1 sweet potato
- 2 carrots
- 3 cloves of garlic
- 2 chillies (red or green)
- 2 tbsp olive oil
- 2 red onions, sliced
- 2 tsp cumin
- 1 tsp cardamom
- 1 tsp turmeric
- 1 tin of green lentils
- 2 vegetable stock cubes
- Salt and pepper
- 1 bag of spinach

METHOD

Chop the sweet potato and carrots into 2 to 3cm chunks. Finely chop the garlic and chillies, removing the seeds if preferred.

Heat the oil in a deep sided frying pan or skillet and then add the onions. Cook for about 5 minutes until they have softened.

Add the garlic and chillies and cook while stirring for another couple of minutes before adding the spices. Cook for another couple of minutes stirring all the time.

Throw in the sweet potato and carrots and cook for another minute or so until they are nicely coated with the spice mixture.

Now add the lentils and enough water to cover everything along with the stock cubes.

Bring to the boil and then turn the heat down and allow the curry to simmer for around 35 to 40 minutes until the vegetables are cooked through.

Add the spinach and stir through for a minute or so until it has wilted.

"Can any of us comprehend what it must be like to run starving from your own home with only the clothes on your back and your children in your arms?"

You can add a sprinkle of coriander or parsley

and then take the pan to the table and serve with rice - enjoy!

"They only want your money
- they don't care if you die."

"I fell in the sea...I thought I would die."

"The boat was punctured
and we fell in the water."

"So I dream to go to Europe. But because
of four years of war in my country no
one will give you papers to come here."

So delicious!

Chicken Satay - African style

Melt in the mouth Congolese Chicken Kebabs -
fire up the barbecue or cook on the grill.

INGREDIENTS

Serves 4

- 4 tbsp peanut butter
- 2 tbsp cayenne pepper
- 1 tbsp smoked paprika
- 1 tbsp garlic powder
- 1 tbsp onion powder
- 1 tsp salt
- 100ml chicken stock (can be a stock cube)
- 800kg boneless and skinless chicken thighs or breast, cut into strips that you can thread onto skewers

METHOD

Take a medium size bowl and mix the peanut butter, all the spices and the salt into the hot stock.

Add the chicken pieces and toss to make sure the chicken is completely covered with the peanut butter sauce.

Leave to marinate for at least 1 hour, or overnight.

Thread the chicken onto long skewers, putting 3 strips of chicken onto each.

The skewers can be cooked on the barbecue. Brush the grill rack with a little oil first to prevent the skewers from sticking, or if preferred you can cook them on a roasting tray in the oven 200°c. Line the baking tray with tin foil and brush the foil with a little oil to prevent sticking.

The chicken is ready when the outside is nice and crispy and the inside is cooked but still nice and juicy. This should take around 20 minutes. Rotate the skewers halfway through the cooking time.

African Chicken Wings

Fire up your
taste buds with
these tasty coated
crispy wings!

INGREDIENTS

Serves 4

- 20 chicken wings
- ½ a lemon, juiced
- 2 cloves of garlic, crushed
- 1 tsp ground black pepper
- 1 tsp ground nutmeg
- 1 tsp smoked paprika
- ½ tsp dried thyme
- 1 tsp ground coriander
- ½ tsp cayenne pepper
- 1 tsp salt
- 120ml yoghurt
- 1 chicken stock cube,
  dissolved in 50ml
  hot water

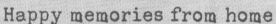

Happy memories from home

METHOD

Put all of the ingredients except the chicken wings into a large bowl and mix well. Add the chicken wings and mix well to coat them all fully.

Leave to marinate in the fridge for at least 1 hour, or overnight if you can.

When you are ready, either cook the wings on the barbecue or under the grill until they are cooked through and the skin is lovely and crispy. Alternatively, pop them in the oven on a grill rack over a roasting tin and cook for 40 to 45 minutes, turning once halfway through the cooking time.

Make sure the skin is crispy and then serve the wings. They work well with the African satay sauce on the previous pages.

"What is at stake is nothing less than the survival and wellbeing of a generation of innocents."
UNHCR

Idris's Story From South Sudan

There are so many stories from people who faced what we cannot start to imagine. One man's story is told below; barely escaping death and torture at the hands of soldiers in Sudan, he made his way to safety in Europe but now, 13 years later, he is still in legal limbo in Greece.

Idris Rohan was working with his father and their driver in the fields one night, when they heard some airplane bombing. This was in the year 2000, and Sudan was in a civil war. Rohan's father went alone to investigate, Rohan followed when he heard more gunfire, and found his father dead, shot in the face by the government militia who seized Rohan and the driver, accusing them of collaborating with the rebels. They were thrown into a lorry full of other people, some of whom were wounded, some dead.

They were kept in an empty school for days, and then eventually Rohan was led into an empty room where they interrogated him, insisting he was working for the rebels. They tied his hands and feet together and hung him from the ceiling, dropping his head into a bucket of water when he gave the wrong answer.

Luckily for Rohan, one of the soldiers holding the rope lost his grip and Rohan dropped to the floor, leaving him badly injured. He was transferred to hospital where one of the nurses was a family friend and helped him escape. He hid in his farmer friends' home for several months while he recovered, before the farmer helped him escape to Lebanon, giving smugglers $4500 to arrange his passage.

His journey to Lebanon was one he wants to forget, but he cannot get rid of the memory. It took a year to cross the vast desert in small groups with the smugglers, in the most extreme

heat and cramped awful conditions before arriving in Siirte, where they had to make the dangerous crossing to Saida. The boat was awful, packed with 75 people; it was just luck they made the crossing. The one the day after didn't, and everyone on board died.

Arriving in Lebanon, Rohan applied for asylum but was rejected. A Sudanese friend helped him get some odd jobs, but without papers he was always worried about police checks, as he would have been sent back home and surely to his death.

Following the progress of other refugees, he decided to take the well-worn path to Greece through Turkey, spending nearly $3000 with smugglers to get there.

The boat crossing was horrendous, taking 6 hours and eventually crashing into rocks off the shallow waters of Lesbos. That was in 2003, and now in 2019 he is still waiting to know if he can stay in Greece. He understands that it is not his country and is still knocking on the door to see if he is allowed in.

Unfortunately, the Greek asylum system just cannot cope with the huge amount of refugees that have arrived in the time Rohan has been there, and the economic situation in Greece is so tough there is no work. He structures his days to try to get through them, waking at 5am to pray, and then spends as much time as he can reading. How he would love to be able to study, to follow his dream of studying veterinary science and then running a cattle and poultry farming station.

Rohan dreams of his homeland but he is haunted by the memories of what happened to his family and friends. 13 years on, this poor man is still in limbo. He still asks himself every night before he falls asleep what he did wrong, and he cannot find the answer.

"Hardships Often Prepare Ordinary People for an Extraordinary Destiny."
C S Lewis

African One Pot Spicy Chicken and Peanut Stew

Our Nigerian family's favourite food.

INGREDIENTS

Serves 4

- 340g smooth peanut butter
- 500ml chicken stock
- 3 tbsp sunflower oil
- 1.6kg bone-in skinless chicken thighs and drumsticks
- 2 onions, thinly sliced
- 4 cloves of garlic, chopped
- 3 tbsp chopped fresh ginger
- 3 chillies, deseeded and chopped
- 3 tsp ground cumin
- 3 tsp ground coriander
- 1 tsp cayenne pepper
- 2 bay leaves
- Salt and black pepper
- 400g tinned chopped tomatoes
- 2 medium size sweet potatoes
- 2 red peppers
- Handful of coriander, chopped

METHOD

Put the peanut butter into a large bowl, add the hot stock and stir them together to make a sauce.

Add 1 tablespoon of the sunflower oil to a very large pan and gently fry the chicken pieces until they are a soft golden colour.

Remove them with a slotted spoon and put them on a plate to rest.

Add the rest of the oil with the onion and fry for about 5 minutes until soft, then add the garlic, ginger, chillies, cumin, coriander, cayenne, bay leaves and a few turns of black pepper. Fry for another 2 minutes.

Pour the peanut sauce into the pan along with the tinned tomatoes and then add the chicken pieces back in. Bring the sauce up to a gentle simmer then put on the lid and simmer for about 30 minutes.

Meanwhile, chop the sweet potatoes into chunks and deseed then chop the peppers. Stir the sweet potatoes, peppers and most of the coriander into the stew and then cook for another 30 minutes with the lid on.

Sprinkle with the remaining coriander and serve!

A Pot of Love and Comfort

Tastes and smells of home in Nigeria
- served and shared with family and friends.

Middle Eastern Herb and Garlic Chicken

If you want a quick and easy crowd pleaser, this chicken is perfect!

Quick and Easy

INGREDIENTS

Serves 4

For the chicken

- 5 cloves of garlic, crushed or grated
- 1 lemon, zested and juiced
- 3 tbsp olive oil
- 1 tsp sea salt
- 1 tbsp sesame seeds
- 3 tbsp za'atar spice mix
- 1 tsp sumac
- 8 skinless and boneless chicken thighs

For the yoghurt

- 120ml Greek yoghurt
- 1 clove of garlic, crushed or grated
- 1 lemon, zested and juiced
- Salt and pepper, to taste

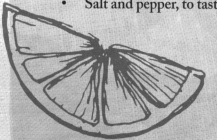

METHOD

Put all the ingredients for the chicken marinade in a large bowl. Mix well before adding the chicken. Make sure the chicken is completely covered all with the marinade; it works well if you use your hands! Cover the bowl and leave in the fridge for at least 1 hour, or overnight if possible.

Grill the marinated chicken on a barbecue. Make sure it is cooked through and has some nice gnarly bits on the outside. Meanwhile, combine all the ingredients for the yoghurt.

When the chicken is ready, pour some of the flavoured yoghurt over the chicken and leave the rest in a bowl for people to help themselves to. This lovely easy dish is great served with a crisp green salad, and it goes well with the tomato and pomegranate salad too.

"'Home sweet home'
is not just a building,
it is the feeling of being part
of a family and community.'

"Think outside the box."

"When it comes to human dignity
we cannot make any compromises."

Refugee Support - Aid with Dignity

Middle Eastern Chicken and Rice

This melt in your mouth chicken dish is bursting with flavour.

INGREDIENTS

Serves 4

- 8 skin on and bone in chicken thighs

For the marinade

- 4 cloves of garlic, crushed
- 2 tbsp freshly squeezed lemon juice
- 2 tbsp turmeric
- 1 tbsp cumin
- ½ tbsp curry powder
- 1 tbsp dried oregano
- 1 tsp salt
- 1 tsp ground black pepper

For the rice

- 2 tbsp olive oil
- 1 red onion, sliced
- 1 clove of garlic, crushed
- 1 tbsp dried oregano
- 1 tsp ground cumin
- 1 tsp tumeric
- 260g basmati rice
- 480ml chicken stock
- 1 tsp salt
- ½ bunch of fresh parsley

METHOD

Put the chicken and the ingredients for the marinade into a large resealable bag and leave to marinate for a minimum of 30 minutes. It's even better if you can leave it overnight to let all those lovely flavours develop. It will smell gorgeous!

Preheat the oven to 200°c. In a large ovenproof skillet or shallow casserole heat half of the olive oil over quite a high heat and then add the chicken, skin side down.

Fry until golden brown - this should take about 5 minutes - then flip them over and repeat on the other side.

Make sure all the chicken looks lovely and brown and crispy before you remove it from the pan. Set that aside on a plate.

Now add the rest of the olive oil to the pot and fry the onion until soft.

Absolutely delicious.

Add the garlic, oregano, cumin and tumeric then sauté for a few minutes.

Add the basmati rice and sauté again for a couple of minutes, stirring all the time until the rice starts to turn a little golden.

Now add the chicken stock and salt, then bring it up to a simmer.

Place the chicken thighs on top of the rice and bring the liquid back up to a simmer.

Cover the pot with a lid and put it in the preheated oven to cook for 30 minutes.

After this time, remove the lid and cook for another 10 to 15 minutes until the liquid has been absorbed, but keep checking so the rice doesn't dry out.

Remove from the oven and sprinkle over some fresh parsley.

Take the pot over to the table and serve with lovely green vegetables and some lemon slices to squeeze over.

Asef from Afghanistan's Story

It was midnight and so so dark when they took us to the beach to get on the boat.

'That's Greece – you have to go towards that light,' they said.

They had taken our money and now were leaving us to make the journey alone.

There were 22 of us, the boat was made for around 5 people.

We set off, petrified.

The waves were huge, and so scary, and the boat broke down halfway across having been at sea for about 3 hours.

Someone was shouting: 'the boat is going soft' and with a sudden huge wave we were submerged. The water was so so cold. I started to choke and believed in all my heart that I would die. So when I saw a light in the distance I couldn't believe God had saved us.

A Turkish police boat had rescued us, but out of the 22 of us that were in the boat, they rescued only 5. The rest had all died.

Irresistible Whole Roasted Potatoes

A great addition to any meal. Let the skins get really crispy and then they really are irresistible!

INGREDIENTS

Serves 4
- 8 medium size potatoes (red skinned are best)
- 8 tbsp olive oil
- Sea salt

METHOD

Preheat the oven to 200°c.

Heat a large pan of boiling water and add the potatoes, then boil for about 15 to 20 minutes until they are nearly cooked through. Drain and let them steam dry until cool enough to handle.

Rub the potatoes all over with the olive oil and then the sea salt. Pop them into a roasting tin, and bake in the oven until they are really crispy and crunchy all over. Naughty but nice!

> "YOUR ENEMY
> IS NOT THE
> REFUGEE; YOUR
> ENEMY IS
> THE ONE WHO
> MADE HIM A
> REFUGEE."
>
> Tariq Ramadan

Cameroon Roasted Fish

Whole roasted barbecued fish: a perfect summer's night supper.

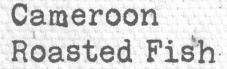

INGREDIENTS

Serves 4

- 2 mackerel or other similar size fish (rainbow trout works well), gutted and cleaned
- 2 tsp salt
- 2 chillies (red or green)
- 1 large onion, peeled
- 1 inch ginger root, peeled
- 6 cloves of garlic, peeled
- 2 stock cubes, vegetable or fish
- 2 tbsp oil
- 12 unsalted peanuts chopped
- 2 spring onions thinely sliced

METHODS

Make a few diagonal lines across each fish, and then sprinkle them with salt, making sure some goes into the cuts.

Roughly chop the chillies, onion, ginger and garlic. Put them into a food processor and blitz. Dissolve the stock cubes in 70ml of hot water, then add to the processor and blend.

Put half of the vegetable paste into a bowl and then rub the rest over the fish, down the cuts and inside the fish as well.

The fish is now ready to grill or barbecue. Put a little oil on the grill to make sure the fish doesn't stick. It should take about 5 minutes on each side to cook until flaky but still moist.

Meanwhile, add the oil to the remaining paste and gently warm in a small saucepan.

To serve the fish sprinkle on the peanuts and spring onions with the sauce on the side.

Yassa Chicken, Gambian Style

The mixture of mustard and chilli really make this dish unique and delicous.

Delicious with potatoes and some green vegetables

METHOD

Trim the excess fat from the chicken, then season with salt and pepper.

Marinate the chicken in half of the onion and garlic mixed with 1 tablespoon of olive oil. Leave for 2 hours, or preferably overnight.

When you are ready to cook, heat the oil in a large deep frying pan and then add the chicken. Cook for about 5 minutes on each side until browned.

Remove the chicken from the pan and set aside.

Add the rest of the oil to the pan and fry the rest of the marinade along with the remaining onion and garlic for 5 minutes until soft. Add the lemon juice, bay leaves, mustard and chilli then cook for another couple of minutes.

Add the chicken back to the pan and pour in the stock. Season with a little salt and pepper then cover and cook for about 20 minutes until the chicken is done throughout.

Check the seasoning, remove the bay leaves and then serve.

Bobo Baldie was a giant of a man, who captured my heart some years ago when he played for my beloved Celtic FC.

In Katiskas camp in Greece there was a lovely group of lads from The Gambia who liked nothing better than to pass the time playing or talking to us about football.

I joked with them about what kind of food Bobo ate to become the 6ft 6 man mountain that he is.

After some discussion, the Gambian boys came up with this delicious Gambian recipe that we are sharing here.

Aya's Story

"I am 32 years old but my hair is totally white; can you imagine walking around after an air raid and seeing human limbs on the ground?"

Aya and her family lived in Al-Qusayr in Syria, but after her brother was captured they ran from Al-Qusayr, leaving their house and all their belongings behind, and moved to her home town, Mheen, to start again. They were farmers, so bought some land and built a house, and for two years were ok.

Then the war came to Mheen so they had to flee again to a further village, but within a few months they were told that Al-Qusayr was safe again, so they returned,

Their house had been burnt to the ground and all their belongings stolen, but they were thankful that they were all safe. "Everything else you can get over." They were safe and that was all that mattered.

Aya and her husband worked so hard, and managed to rebuild everything, but within a few months armed groups came back to their town. The situation was just a huge mess, no one knew which group was fighting for which reason, they were so lost and didn't even know who was right and who was wrong.

"I cannot tell you the suffering and hardship we went through during these years - it's inexplicable."

Aya had one daughter but suffered multiple miscarriages due to the shock and stresses she faced daily. Then one day, when she was at her relative's house, not more than 10 metres from her own house, the fighting was so intense and so close, they had no choice but to run immediately and in the chaos, panic and confusion Aya and her daughter got separated from her husband who ran the other way.

"We honestly believed that if you had nothing to do with the war, nothing would happen to you, but we were wrong, so wrong."

They travelled for 5 hours into the desert, where they had to stay for 5 months, hoping their village would be safe again and they could return. Eventually they lost hope, so followed the rest of the displaced people to the Jordanian border. Aya was with strangers and had no idea what was going to happen to her and her daughter.

The journey was perilous. One day, entering a village, people were standing in line at a local bakery where, out of nowhere, there was air strike which directly hit the bakery. In front of her eyes Aya saw over 25 people die, most of them children.

She saw a woman losing her two children in that air raid, who was standing a few metres from where the bomb struck, and she was watching them die in shock, just standing there.

Aya arrived in Jordan, and after two months of being there and having no news of her husband, someone showed her a photo of him on Facebook with a caption that declared his death.

"I have to try to live for my daughter but I have nothing."

"My life in Syria was wonderful, I was living in a beautiful green village, I was living in freedom. We used to visit our family and friends' houses to spend evenings and have fun. All this was taken away. My husband was wonderful, he gave me everything. He loved me and treated me with the utmost respect, if only he could see me now. I cannot work, I don't even have enough money to buy my daughter a cookie, I don't have a single lira to buy her anything. I feel so helpless and heartbroken."

"To be called a refugee is the opposite of an insult; it is a badge of strength, courage and victory."

Relaxed and Easy One Pot Middle Eastern Fish Stew

Fish in a pot with subtle spices from the Middle East, to be shared with family and friends.

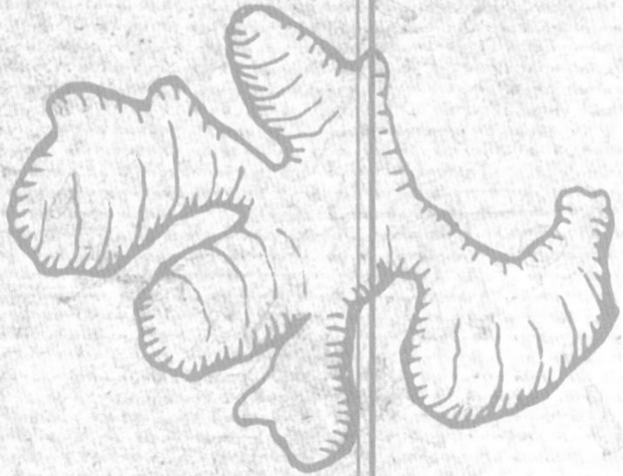

INGREDIENTS
Serves 4

- 1 tbsp olive oil
- 1 onion, thinly sliced
- 1 clove of garlic, crushed
- 2 tsp fresh ginger, grated
- 1 tsp ground cumin
- 1 tsp turmeric
- 1 cinnamon stick
- 250ml fish stock
- 400g tinned chopped tomatoes
- Salt and black pepper
- 500g white fish fillets (cod, snapper, haddock)
- 400g tinned chickpeas
- Fresh coriander leaves (optional)

METHOD

Heat the olive oil in a large heavy-based pan and then add the onion and fry, stirring frequently, for about 5 minutes until the onion is soft and translucent.

Add the garlic, ginger, cumin, turmeric and cinnamon stick. Cook for 2 minutes, stirring regularly.

Add the fish stock, tomatoes and a pinch of salt then cook for another 10 minutes, stirring occasionally. Meanwhile, cut the fish into chunks

Add the chickpeas and the fish then cook for around 5 minutes until the fish is just cooked through. It should be nice and soft and flaky. Taste the stew, adding salt and pepper as necessary.

Take the pan off the heat and sprinkle some coriander leaves over the stew if you like, then take it to the table in the pan.

"No mother would put her children on a boat unless the water was safer than the land they were fleeing from."
Warsan Shire

Tabbouleh is lovely with this too!

Mouthwatering Grilled Salmon with North African Flavours

Perfect for the barbecue, but if it's too cold outside, this is also a lovely and easy recipe to do under the grill.

INGREDIENTS

Serves 4

For the herb paste

- 4 tbsp plain yoghurt
- 3 tbsp chopped parsley
- 3 tbsp chopped coriander
- 3 cloves of garlic, crushed
- 2 tbsp lemon juice
- 1 tbsp extra-virgin olive oil
- 1 tsp paprika
- 1 tsp ground cumin
- Salt and pepper, to taste
- 4 pieces of salmon, skinned

METHOD

Mix all the ingredients for the herb paste together in a large bowl.

Add the salmon and coat all over with the sauce, turning it a few times to make sure it is coated well.

Leave to marinate for 30 minutes while you preheat the grill or light the barbecue.

Once the grill is hot, add the salmon and cook for about 5 minutes on each side until lightly browned and only just cooked in the middle.

Serve with wedges of lemon, some rice or new potatoes.

Zara's Story

Zara and Ahmad and their lovely family fled Iraq to seek refuge and safety in Europe.

They travelled first from Iraq through to Turkey, and then on to Greece, arriving at Lesbos and then on to Katsikas camp.

They have been in Greece now for almost a year, and have no idea how long they will be in Katsikas. It is another 3 months until they have their next appointment to discuss their asylum.

What struck us most was how happy and grateful they were, so positive about the long term future and appreciative of everything that was being done to support them.

Zara was so enthusiastic to help and share her recipe from home, and what fun we had learning about it.

Zara's Amazing Iraqi Chicken and Rice

When you cook this wonderful aromatic dish, think of the bustling markets and colours of the Middle East. The flavours just burst in your mouth.

INGREDIENTS

Serves 4

- Oil for cooking (olive if possible)
- 1 whole chicken, cut into pieces
- 1 lemon
- 2 onions
- 1 tsp curry powder
- 1 tsp turmeric
- 1 tsp ginger
- 2 tsp salt
- 1 chicken stock cube
- 2 handfuls of vermicelli
- 3 cups of rice
- ½ lemon, juiced
- ½ tsp cardamom

METHOD

Take a huge saucepan – as big as you can find – heat up 3 tablespoons of oil in it, then add the chicken pieces and fry until they are lovely and brown all over.

Cut the lemon into slices and add them to the pan.

Cut the onions into chunks and throw them in, then add the spices, except the cardamon, the salt and the stock cube. Stir so everything is covered in the wonderful spices. Leave to simmer.

Crush the vermicelli into small pieces, then heat 4 tablespoons of oil in a seperate pan. Fry the vermicelli in the oil until brown.

Add this to the chicken along with 3 cups of water and the rice. Put the lid on and cook for 1 hour. With 10 minutes of cooking time left, add the lemon juice and the cardamom, and give it all a good stir. Pop the lid back on for the final 10 minutes and then it is ready to share at the table.

Eat and enjoy!

"Refugees Have No Choice - You Do."

A Syrian child refugee
- why we had to leave

"The war started in 2011. This was the year I stopped going to school as my school was bombed - four children died.

A few days later the terrorists came to the town where we lived, with machine guns and bombs.

There were bodies and blood all over the streets, we hid in our house.

The terrorists gave us two hours to leave the area if we didn't want to die, we grabbed small bags and ran.

We stayed in Syria for a further three years. Each place we moved to eventually the terrorists came, and the city would be bombed. We stayed with my auntie for six months, until they came here too, bombs landing every five or six minutes. We moved to my grandmother's house and the same happened. Eventually we went to find my uncle's house but by the time we got there it was too late, it had been bombed and was covered with blood. My mother said there was now no choice, we had to leave Syria to save our lives, so we left and began our tortuous journey.

Try to imagine
losing your home,
your occupation, your
friends, your family and
everything familiar that
we all take for granted.

Try to imagine being a refugee.

Ali's Story
Ali - 34 from Iran

Ali was one of the most articulate and inspirational of all the young refugees we were privileged to spend time with as volunteers for Refugee Support.

"Refugees are mothers, fathers, sisters, brothers, children with the same hopes and ambitions as us - fate has dealt them this hand."

Ali describes himself as a philosopher and humanitarian. He had been a very successful business marketing manager and also worked for the government while living in his homeland, Iran.

We met him in Cyprus when he had come to the Refugee Council to help translate for a group of refugees who were living in the Kofinu camp, where he too was living in awful conditions. He was a refugee, as his outspoken humanitarian views and observations had resulted in him not being able to safely return to Iran.

Ali and his wife had left Iran 3 years earlier; their plan had been to travel to 200 countries exploring and spreading his thoughts and humanitarian ideals. They were unable to travel to all but a few countries; coming from Iran they were refused entry, Ali's reply being "I come from Iran - am I a criminal?"

His positivity was infectious as he explained to the new refugees that it was likely to take a year or more for them to gain refugee status and urged them to seize this opportunity to have the time to learn new skills, languages or interests that would help them be better prepared to adapt to whatever they may wish to do in the future. He called it "a chance to be born again".

Ghormeh Sabzi
Persian Herb Stew

This tasty recipe is from the beautiful Azita, Ali's wife. She told me that it is the most delicious food in Iran, and it really is so good. I had never used dried limes before, but they do add a completely different flavour, and are well worth the extra effort.

INGREDIENTS

Serves 4
- 250g mixture of fresh herbs, leeks and spinach
- 7 tbsp oil
- 1 yellow onion, finely chopped
- 500g lamb, cubed
- 1 tsp turmeric
- 500ml water
- 400g tinned kidney beans
- 3 dried limes
- Salt and pepper

METHOD

Wash the herbs and vegetables then chop everything finely. You can use a food processor for this.

Put a large dry saucepan on a low heat and sauté the veggies and herbs for about 10 minutes until they dry out a little, then add 4 tablespoons of oil and fry on a low heat for 10 to 15 minutes.

Transfer the softened vegetables and herbs to a plate until needed.

Heat the remaining oil in the pan, add the onion and fry until light brown. Add the lamb and the turmeric then fry for another 3 to 4 minutes.

Add the water and kidney beans to the pot and bring the stew to the boil.

Turn the heat down and leave to simmer for 1 hour with the lid on. Then add the vegetable and herb mixture and simmer for another hour.

Pierce the limes with a skewer about 4 times each and then add them to the stew. Continue to simmer for 1 hour.

Remove the lid, add salt and pepper to taste and turn up the heat to let the excess water evaporate.

It is then ready to be served with white rice, but if you can wait it tastes even better the next day!

Jewelled rice

So good, so easy!

Gorgeous colourful rice, full of
textures and flavours. In Iran they
serve this at weddings and banquets but
it's lovely for every day meals too.

INGREDIENTS

Serves 4

- 100g dried cranberries
- 100g raisins or currants
- Knob of butter, for frying
- 50g pistachios
- 50g almonds
- 2 carrots, peeled and grated
- Peel of 1 large orange
- 1 large onion, peeled and chopped
- 2 tsp ground cinnamon
- 1 tsp ground cardamom
- 600g basmati rice
- ½ tsp saffron, steeped in 2 tbsp boiling water
- Rose petals, for decorating
- Salt and black pepper, to taste

METHOD

Fry the cranberries and raisins in a little butter and then add the nuts and fry for a few minutes. Add the carrots and orange peel, then add the onion and fry until softened. Stir in the ground spices.

Cook the rice according to the instructions on the packet. Just before it has finished cooking, add the saffron.

Tip the rice into a serving dish and scatter the nuts and fruit over the top, then add the rose petals. You can lay the different elements out in strips for effect.

"Human suffering anywhere concerns men and women everywhere."
- Elie Wiesel

Samuel and his family fled their home when men with machetes attacked their village in the Democratic Republic of Congo.

"They looted and burnt down everything in their way, killing men, women and children", said the 32 year old.

Samuel, his wife and three young children spent months in a nearby town, sleeping outside, without enough food or water. The conditions were so unbearable the couple decided to send their older children to live with their grandmother in a neighbouring village, so they could go back home to see if it was safe to return. They found the village destroyed, their house reduced to ashes.

Samuel and his wife were rebuilding their lives when they were attacked again.

"Going back to the bush was not an option anymore."

Samuel's account reflects that of scores of refugees and asylum seekers arriving in Uganda with little more than the clothes on their backs. All tell stories of brutality at the hands of armed groups going from village to village, looting, burning houses, killing men, women and children.

At this time Uganda has over 1.2 million refugees.

"Refugees are not numbers, they are people who have faces, names, stories, and need to be treated as such."
- Pope Francis

Herb and Nut Crusted Salmon
From the Middle East: decadent but delicious!

INGREDIENTS

Serves 4
- 1 side of salmon
- 2 tbsp coconut oil
- Salt and pepper
- ½ lemon, juiced
- 2 tsp ground cumin
- 2 cloves of garlic, crushed
- 2 tbsp tahini paste
- 1 lemon, sliced

For the crust
- 1 red onion, peeled and chopped
- 2 large handfuls of fresh coriander, leaves only
- 2 large handfuls of fresh flat leaf parsley, leaves only
- 1 handful of fresh mint, leaves only
- 3 red chillies
- 60g almonds, finely chopped
- 10g walnuts, finely chopped
- 2 tbsp sumac

Sometimes the most delicious things
can be the most simple, yet this
dish looks so impressive!

METHOD

Preheat the oven to 140°c. Rub the coconut oil all over the salmon and then season with salt and pepper.

Loosely wrap the salmon in baking paper, twisting the ends to seal the parcel, then place on a baking tray.

Bake the salmon in the preheated oven for about 20 minutes, then turn the oven off and leave it to cool in there.

While the salmon cools, combine the lemon juice, cumin, garlic and tahini in a small bowl. Mix to form a paste; you may need to add a couple of tablespoons of water.

Make the herb crust by putting all the ingredients into a food processor and blitz until the consistency is spreadable.

Unwrap the salmon and spread the tahini dressing all over the top side, and then cover that with the herb crust.

Sprinkle with a few coriander leaves and decorate with slices of lemon.

Enjoy!

Super African Vitality Burger

Who needs meat when a veggie burger can taste this good. This African style super tasty chickpea burger has been inspired by conversations with our lovely refugee friend Abraham.

INGREDIENTS

Serves 4

- 2 tbsp olive oil, plus extra for frying
- 1 onion, finely chopped
- 1 clove of garlic, crushed
- 225g carrots, coarsely grated
- 2 medium courgettes, finely diced
- 400g tinned chickpeas, drained and rinsed
- 2 tbsp crunchy peanut butter
- 1 egg yolk
- 3 tsp korma curry paste
- 3 tbsp fresh parsley
- 80g fresh wholemeal breadcrumbs
- Salt and black pepper, to taste

For serving

- 4 bread rolls
- 4 tbsp mayonnaise, mixed with 2 tbsp chopped fresh coriander
- 2 tomatoes, thinly sliced

METHOD

Take a large deep frying pan and heat the oil. Add the onion and fry for around 5 minutes until it has softened.

Add the garlic, carrots and courgettes and fry for 5 minutes until everything has softened. Set aside to cool.

Put the chickpeas into a food processor and blend until smooth, then tip into a large mixing bowl. Add the peanut butter, egg yolk, curry paste and parsley and stir well before adding the cooled vegetables and breadcrumbs. Mix well and season to taste.

Shape the mixture into 4" (10 cm) flat discs. If you have a metal pastry cutter this size, shaping the patties is much easier. They should be about 2cm deep. Cover and chill for 2 hours if possible.

Brush the chilled burgers with a little oil and then they are ready to either fry or grill. If you are frying them, heat a frying pan over a medium heat then place the burgers in for about 5 minutes each side. They should have a golden crispy coating.

If you are using a barbecue they will take about 6 minutes each side.

To serve, split the rolls in half, put coriander mayonnaise on both halves then put the burgers in and top with a couple of tomato slices.

Abraham's Story

The full story, as told by 26-year-old Abraham from Cameroon when we met him at the Refugee Support Dignity Centre in Cyprus.

"My name is Tabot Abraham and I am from Cameroon.

The reason I am a refugee is because of the major crisis in my country. My father was a military officer and he was sent by the government to fight against his own people.

He refused to do this so the military were sent to his house. They tied my mother and father to a post inside their house then set fire to it. This is how my parents were killed.

I found them like this and I just had to run for my life.

I have a sister and two brothers but I don't know where they are.

I am in Cyprus now as a refugee seeking asylum, as it is not safe for me to return to Cameroon.

I really want to be able to build a new life for me and to help others also."

"Try to see things through someone else's eyes."

Barbecued Leg of Lamb
with Yoghurt and Saffron Marinade

The way that this lamb is cooked on the
barbecue makes it so succulent and juicy. We
cannot recommend it enough! It's a great meal
to share with friends and family; the whole
leg should do about 6 people.

INGREDIENTS

Serves 6

- 1 whole leg of lamb, boned and butterflied
- 3 cloves of garlic, crushed
- 1 tsp cumin seeds, gently toasted in a dry pan for a few minutes and then ground with a pestle and mortar or 1 tsp ground cumin
- 5 sprigs of thyme, leaves picked and chopped finely
- 100g Greek yoghurt
- ½ tsp saffron, steeped in 1 tsp water
- 1 lemon, zested and juiced
- 1 tsp smoked paprika
- 2 tbsp extra-virgin olive oil
- Sea salt and freshly ground black pepper

Could serve with a Middle Eastern salad and some batata hara.

METHOD

It's a really good idea to prepare the lamb the day before you want to cook it, as the flavours really develop.

The marinade is very simple to make. Combine the garlic, cumin, thyme and yoghurt. Mix well before adding the saffron, paprika, lemon juice, zest and olive oil.

Rub the lamb all over, on both sides, with the marinade and then pop in the fridge for at least 2 hours, preferably overnight.

The next day, cook the lamb on the barbecue for around 20 minutes each side. It's nice to get some lovely gnarled bits on the outside and beautifully pink in the middle.

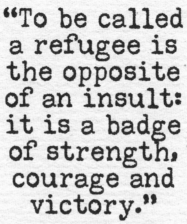

> "To be called a refugee is the opposite of an insult: it is a badge of strength, courage and victory."
>
> Tennessee Office for Refugees

Ali, a child from Iraq

News of war was always on the radio; he heard how Daesh kills people: old, young, women and men, killed or captured.

"We knew what they were capable of, and we knew what we were to do. When Daesh arrives - you need to run. When early one morning we heard shooting in the village and people shouting 'Daesh are coming' I ran home as fast as I could to look for my mother, but I couldn't find her anywhere, the only thing I could do was to run, I did and I left without her. I have no idea if she is dead or alive".

Hara Batara Middle Eastern skillet potatoes

Naughty but nice, a bundle of tasty crispness – so moreish!

INGREDIENTS

Serves 4

- 6 medium potatoes, peeled and chopped into bite-size pieces
- 3 tbsp extra-virgin olive oil
- 2 cloves of garlic, crushed
- 1 tsp ground coriander
- 1 tsp crushed red pepper flakes
- 2 tsp turmeric
- 1 lime, juiced
- Bunch of coriander leaves
- Bunch of parsley leaves
- 3 tbsp chopped dill

METHOD

Put the potatoes into a large pan of salted water and bring to the boil. Cook for around 10 to 15 minutes until they are cooked through but still firm, then drain them and leave to cool a little.

Heat the olive oil in a large heavy-bottomed frying pan. Add the garlic, coriander and red pepper flakes. Cook for a few minutes before adding the turmeric and lime juice.

Add the potatoes and mix well to make sure they are coated with the spices and fry for a few minutes, letting the potatoes brown.

Add the coriander leaves, parsley and dill with some salt and pepper to taste. Cook for another 5 minutes, making sure the potatoes are crispy and brown all over.

Serve straight from the pan.

It's universally recognised –
you can never have too many crispy potatoes

Chicken and Potato Bangladeshi Curry

This curry has just the right amount of spice; it gives you a warm feeling but doesn't blow your brains out!

INGREDIENTS

Serves 4

- 1 tsp turmeric
- 1 tsp cayenne pepper
- 2 tsp salt
- 1 kg boneless and skinless chicken thighs
- 3 medium potatoes, peeled then diced into bite-size pieces
- 3 tsp cumin seeds
- 1 tsp coriander seeds
- 1 tsp dried red chilli flakes
- 3 tbsp oil (can be grapeseed, olive or any vegetable oil)
- 1 large onion, sliced
- 1 tbsp grated ginger
- 2 cloves of garlic, crushed
- 2 green chillies, finely diced
- 2 fresh tomatoes, diced
- 2 bay leaves
- 3 tbsp chopped fresh coriander

"Overcrowding is inhuman in the Moira Camp, Lesvos, Greece.

25 women sleep in a tent with a single bathroom.

It is filthy but we wash in it anyway as we have no alternative."

METHOD

Put the turmeric, salt and cayenne pepper in a mixing bowl, combine and then add the chicken. Mix well so the chicken is covered with the spices.

Put the potatoes into a small pan of boiling water and cook for 5 to 10 minutes until they are almost cooked, then take off the heat, drain and set aside.

Grind the cumin and coriander seeds with the chilli flakes in a spice grinder or pestle and mortar until smooth.

Put the oil into a large deep frying pan and heat before adding the onion. Fry for about 5 minutes until soft, then add the ginger, garlic and chillies and fry for another couple of minutes before adding the chicken. Fry for a few minutes, stirring as you go, until the chicken is a lovely golden brown.

Add the ground cumin, coriander and chilli to the pan and fry everything for another couple of minutes.

Add the potatoes, tomatoes, bay leaves and about 150ml of water. Bring gently to the boil, then cover, turn the heat down to a gentle simmer and cook for about 10 minutes until the tomatoes have completely softened.

Add salt and pepper to taste and sprinkle with the fresh coriander.

This is ready to serve with rice, fresh naan or chapatis.

> "No one has ever become poor by giving."
> — Anne Frank

Peanut, Sweet Potato and Kale Vegan Stew

This West African styled stew is insanely comforting and delicious, great for everyone whether you're vegan or not.

INGREDIENTS

Serves 4

- 6 cloves of garlic
- 3cm root ginger, peeled and chopped
- 2 green chillies, deseeded and thinly sliced
- Small bunch of coriander
- Salt and pepper
- 3 tbsp olive oil
- 1 tsp turmeric
- 6 spring onions, thinly sliced
- 2 tins of coconut milk
- 1 litre vegetable stock
- 2 large or 4 small sweet potatoes, diced into bite-size pieces
- 200g shelled peanuts
- 150g kale, roughly chopped and thick stems removed
- 2 limes, juiced
- 2 tbsp hot sauce (optional)

METHOD

Put the garlic, ginger, one of the chillies, the coriander stems (keep the leaves) and 1 teaspoon of salt into a pestle and mortar. Pound until the mixture has become a thick paste.

Heat 2 tablespoons of oil in a large saucepan and add the paste. Fry this while stirring for a minute or so and then add the turmeric and half of the spring onions. Cook for another minute.

Add the coconut milk, vegetable stock and the sweet potatoes. Bring the stew up to the boil and then reduce to a bare simmer. Cook for about 15 minutes.

Meanwhile, put the peanuts in a frying pan with the remaining oil. Cook these while tossing frequently. You want them to brown all over but not to burn! This should take about 8 minutes.

Once they are ready roughly chop about 10 of the peanuts to use for garnish. Put the rest into the pestle and

mortar with a pinch of salt and pound them to a rough paste. Add this to the stew.

Once the sweet potatoes are cooked through, blend everything with a stick blender. Bring the stew back to the boil, then turn down to a simmer and add the kale. Allow this to cook until it is completely wilted, which should take 5 to 8 minutes.

Stir in the lime juice then add salt and pepper to taste.

You can now add as much hot sauce as you like, if you are using it.

Roughly chop the coriander leaves then add these to the stew, leaving a few aside to sprinkle on the top.

Serve the stew with rice, and sprinkle with the remaining chopped peanuts, spring onions, sliced chillies and coriander leaves.

> "We have a legal and moral obligation to protect people fleeing bombs, bullets and tyrants, and throughout history those people have enriched our society."
> - Juliet Stevenson

"How can it be right that refugees who have fled the most horrendous situations imaginable are then left in limbo for up to two years while their applications are processed?"

Beatrice's Sizzling Peri Peri Chicken Somalian Style

This tongue-tingling chicken has been inspired by Beatrice, one of the lovely refugees we met, who is from Somalia. This dish is brimming with flavour.

INGREDIENTS

Serves 4

- 1 red onion, roughly chopped
- 2 green chillies
- 3 cloves of garlic
- 4 basil leaves
- 1 tbsp fresh oregano
- 4 tbsp olive oil
- 120ml coconut milk
- 1 chicken stock cube, dissolved in 50ml water
- 1 tsp smoked paprika
- 1 lemon, juiced
- ½ tsp salt
- Black pepper, to taste
- 2kg chicken thighs

METHOD

To make the marinade, put the onion, chillies, garlic, basil and oregano in a food processor and blend.

Add the olive oil and coconut milk, to the processor, then the chicken stock, paprika, lemon juice and salt. Add black pepper then pour the marinade into a sealable plastic bag.

Trim the chicken thighs and then rub all over with salt and pepper.

So good, so easy!

Add them to the bag with the marinade in. Toss and swizzle the chicken in the bag until it is completely covered with the marinade, then pop in the fridge overnight if possible, or at least for a couple of hours.

If you are cooking the chicken in an oven, preheat it to 200°c and then roast for about 40 minutes, turning half way through, until it is cooked, brown and crispy. If you using a barbecue it will take the same amount of time, but make sure you turn the chicken a few times while cooking so it cooks evenly.

"Refugee problems don't finish when the reporters leave. They are stuck and cannot go back to where they came from."

Jude's Story

We met Jude in Cyprus when we were helping Refugee Support set up their amazing Dignity Centre in the heart of Nicosia.

A local church group were running a breakfast club for the refugees sleeping rough.

Jude was one of these young men that you were just drawn to. He had only just arrived in Cyprus and was clearly tired, shaken and alone.

Jude slept on the floor of a church with over 30 others in a similar position.

Conditions were not good but he was so grateful for the little he had been given and was appreciative of the hand of friendship the volunteers and local community were able to offer.

This is Jude's story as told to us.

"I left Nigeria in March 2019 and after a long and tough journey finally arrived in Cyprus over a month later at the end of April. I thank God I came through.

Earlier, around 6th to 8th March, there were serious Boko Haram attacks in some of the major towns of Mafa, a local government area of Borno state.

My family is comprised of my parents and my three sisters who live in Mafa town in Borno, Nigeria.

On that fateful day I was at my business place, both my parents should have been at my home and my immediate younger sister went to work while my two kid sisters went to school.

Without any warning there was shooting everywhere, people running here and there and some houses were on fire. From my business place to my house was 30 minutes by foot. I ran home only to find out that the house was empty, everyone in the vicinity had also fled from their homes. I managed to escape the area and jumped into a drainage. I dislocated my left ankle but I kept running and hiding from one spot to the other. The shooting was really heavy and a lot of people died in the process but God kept me safe. I ran into a man called Alhaji, who was one of my customers. He is a Muslim man and well connected, so offered to hide me. I hid for two weeks but I could not find my parents or my sisters even though I tried to phone them all every single day but nothing available on their phones, even till this day their phones are not available.

Alhaji offered to help me leave Nigeria because there was no hope for me to stay alive. I had no choice than to accept his offer and after such tough travel found myself in North Cyprus where I was stranded for three weeks before, after great difficulty, managing to cross over to the Republic of Cyprus where I hope to seek asylum and safe life."

"Remember every **child's smile** is precious."

"As humans it's a joy to witness so many different cultures living together in harmony."

Spicy Chicken with Harissa and Lentils

When you're looking for something easy with little fuss but lots of flavour, this could be the recipe for you. It only takes minutes to prepare!

INGREDIENTS

Serves 4

- 2-3 tbsp olive oil
- 1 red onion, sliced into half moons
- 2 cloves of garlic, crushed
- 3 tbsp harissa
- 8 chicken thighs, skinned and boned
- 1 carrot, grated
- 200g Puy lentils
- 800g tinned chopped tomatoes
- 1 litre chicken stock
- Chopped flat leaf parsley, for garnishing

METHOD

Heat the olive oil in a large frying pan and fry the onion for around 5 minutes until soft, then add the garlic and fry for a further minute.

Stir in the harissa, then add the chicken and fry until browned all over.

Stir in the carrot, lentils and tomatoes, then add the stock and bring to the boil.

Reduce the heat and cook uncovered for around 45 minutes. By this time most of the liquid will have been absorbed by the lentils.

Add salt and pepper to taste and then sprinkle on the flat leaf parsley.

Serve with a simple green vegetable like peas or beans. Terrific!

"Happiness creeps up on you when you least expect it."

"The cure for unhappiness is happiness."

> ## "You can't put a price on a smile or a hug from a stranger."

West African Shrimp (Prawns!)

Mildly spiced but full of flavour, this simple dish is absolutely heavenly.

INGREDIENTS

Serves 4

- 1 tbsp cumin seeds
- 2 tsp coriander seeds
- 1 tbsp olive oil
- 1 red onion, finely sliced
- 3 cloves of garlic, crushed
- 1 tbsp hot paprika
- ½ tsp cayenne pepper
- 4 large tomatoes, diced
- 100ml fish stock
- ½ tin of coconut milk
- 30-35 raw prawns, peeled
- ½ lemon, juiced
- Fresh coriander, chopped

METHOD

In a large frying pan, dry fry the cumin and coriander seeds, stirring often until you can smell the beautiful aroma as they heat up. Grind the spices to a powder with a pestle and mortar.

Heat the oil in the same pan and fry the onion until soft and translucent. Add the garlic, ground seeds, paprika, and cayenne pepper.

Fry for a couple of minutes then add the tomatoes and fish stock.

Leave the sauce to cook down on a medium heat for around 15 minutes until the tomatoes have broken down.

Add the coconut milk, and once this is warm add the prawns. These should only take about 5 minutes to cook through.

Once the prawns have turned pink, add the lemon juice and sprinkle with a little fresh coriander, then you are ready to serve.

Cameroon Vegetable Jollof Rice

Jollof rice is made in every household in West Africa, each family having their own version passed down from generation to generation.

This version is from Cameroon, taken from a conversation with Joseph, one of the lovely boys we met in Cyprus. Now living in a church, sleeping on the floor along with 20 other men, waiting to know if he will get asylum, he dreamt of happier days at home and told me about how his grandmother and mother cooked this rice dish for everyone.

INGREDIENTS

Serves 4
- 4 cloves of garlic
- 2cm ginger, peeled and finely chopped
- 1 stick of celery, diced
- 1 chilli (red or green)
- 3 large tomatoes
- 3 tsbp vegetable oil
- 1 onion, diced
- 1 green pepper, chopped
- 1 spring onion, chopped
- 1 carrot, diced
- 3 vegetable stock cubes
- 150g tomato purée
- 200g rice
- 1 tsp curry powder
- 1 tsp salt
- 10 green beans, chopped
- 2 sprigs of coriander, finely chopped

METHOD

Put the garlic, ginger, celery and chilli into a blender. Blitz to chop well before adding the tomatoes and 150ml of water, then blend the mixture into a purée.

Put the oil in a large saucepan and fry the onion for around 5 minutes, or until soft and translucent.

Add the green pepper, spring onion and carrot then fry for a couple more minutes.

Add the stock cubes, blended tomatoes and tomato purée to the pan. Stir well and leave to simmer.

At the same time, put the rice in a separate saucepan, add the curry powder and salt then cook in boiling water until just tender. When the rice is ready, drain off any excess water and then keep it warm with a lid on.

Keep cooking the spiced sauce slowly, stirring occasionally, and after about 5 minutes add the green beans. Cook for a further 5 minutes.

Add the rice to the sauce and mix on a low heat until everything is well incorporated. Taste the jollof then add salt and pepper as necessary.

Sprinkle with the chopped coriander to garnish and serve.

Cameroonian refugees flee to find safety

When armed men swept into her village in north-west Cameroon, mother of four Jasmine only had time to gather up her children and run.

'I could not take anything. There was shooting - they killed my uncle and shot my cousin.'

As she fled into the bush, gunmen shot her husband dead. As she hid, she saw the armed men douse their house in petrol and set it alight.

In another village, 22-year-old Krista looked on as gun-toting men stormed into her village and opened fire.

'Stray bullets sprayed everywhere - people were being shot indiscriminately,' says Krista, who escaped into the bush with her family. She hid in the bush, unable to return for fear of being shot.'

Jasmine and Krista are among the 26,000 civilians who have fled the south-west and north-west regions of Cameroon and sought safety in Nigeria.

They are praying for a happier future and hope they will one day be able to return home to Cameroon.

Middle Eastern Roasted Salmon with Lemony Chickpea Couscous

This mouthwatering Middle Eastern dish is very easy to prepare, and any leftovers are just as good in your lunchbox the next day.

You can make this recipe following option one or two: if you're short of time the first part can be skipped and the end result is still delicious.

INGREDIENTS

Serves 6 (with some leftovers!)
For Option 1
- 2 tbsp olive oil
- 1 onion, finely diced
- 1 small fennel bulb, finely sliced
- 1 clove of garlic, crushed
- 1 tsp cumin seeds
- 1 lemon, zested

For Option 2
- 1 tbsp honey
- 1 tbsp harissa
- 1 side of salmon

- 1 lemon, sliced

For the couscous
- 200g couscous or bulgar wheat
- 1 vegetable stock cube
- 400g tinned chickpeas
- 50g currants
- 1 lemon, zested and juiced
- Bunch of flat leaf parsley, chopped
- Bunch of mint, chopped
- 2 tsp harissa
- 50g flaked almonds, toasted

METHOD

Start here for Option 1
Heat the oil in a frying pan then add the onion, fennel, garlic and cumin seeds. Fry for about 15 minutes until everything is soft and golden, then stir in the lemon zest, add some salt and pepper to taste and leave to cool.

Start here for Option 2
Mix the honey and harissa together. Place the salmon skin side down on baking paper and spread the top with the honey and harissa mixture.

Option 1
Cut the side of salmon in half, place the pieces skin side down and spread the top of the larger piece with some of the honey and harissa mixture. Now spread the fried onion and fennel mixture over that, then place the second half of the salmon on top and spread the remaining honey and harissa mixture on the top piece of salmon.

Option 1 and 2

Either preheat the oven to 180°c or light the barbecue. Place the salmon on the barbecue to cook for about 20 minutes, or place it onto a baking sheet and cook in the oven for 20 minutes. Check the fish is cooked all the way through; it should look opaque and flake easily without being dry.

For the couscous or bulgar wheat

Cook the bulgar wheat or couscous according to the instructions on the packet, adding the vegetable stock cube.

Just before it is ready, add the chickpeas, currants, lemon zest and juice, parsley, mint and harissa to the coucous or blugar wheat. Stir well to warm everything through. Add the toasted flaked almonds and stir well.

Take a big platter and spread the couscous over it, then place the salmon on the top. Sprinkle with some chopped parsley and finish with a few slices of lemon before serving.

Bangladeshi Mushroom and Pea Curry

A real 'whack it all in a pot' type of recipe, this lovely vegan recipe is brimming with flavour. Go wild, shed your inhibitions and try it!

INGREDIENTS

Serves 4

- 2 tbsp oil
- 1 onion, sliced into half moons
- 3 cloves of garlic, finely chopped
- 3 green chillies, 1 deseeded then finely chopped and 2 left whole but slit up the side
- 1 tsp mustard seeds
- 1 tsp turmeric
- 1 tsp chilli powder

- 400g mushrooms
- 6 large tomatoes, chopped
- 400ml vegetable stock
- 1 lemon, juiced
- 200g frozen petit pois
- 1 red chilli, deseeded and finely sliced (for garnish)
- Some chopped coriander (for garnish)

METHOD

Heat the oil in a large deep frying pan.

Fry the onions until soft and translucent, then add the garlic, chopped green chilli, mustard seeds, turmeric and chilli powder. Continue to cook for another 3 minutes.

Add the mushrooms and fry until they have started to colour. This should take 3 to 4 minutes.

Then add the chopped tomatoes, the whole chillies, and the vegetable stock. Bring to the boil then turn down the heat, add the lemon juice and allow the sauce to simmer away, reducing it slightly to intensify the flavours.

Once the tomatoes are no longer lumpy, the curry will be ready, after about 15 minutes of simmering. Stir in the peas, sprinkle with red chilli and coriander then serve with basmati rice.

"We hope to provide aid with dignity, and a world without borders."

Basmati rice is all you need to complement this simple but tasty curry!

The shakshuka of the North African fish world
Fish Chraymeh

Tantalising, spicy and totally gorgeous!

INGREDIENTS

- *Serves 4*
- 4 tbsp vegetable oil (rapeseed or olive is best)
- 2 red chillies, deseeded and finely chopped
- 2 red peppers, finely sliced
- 5 cloves of garlic, finely chopped
- 1 tbsp sweet paprika
- 2 tsp cumin seeds, toasted
- 4 tbsp aniseed spirit (such as Pernod or ouzo)
- 1 tbsp harissa
- 100ml water
- 400g tinned tomatoes
- Pinch of sugar
- 4 cod fillets (or similar fish)
- Large bunch of coriander, chopped
- Squeeze of lemon juice
- 3 tsp hawaij spice mix (optional but fab – see page 158 for how to make this)

One big pot of loveliness to share

METHOD

Heat up the oil in a large pot, then add the chillies and red peppers. Fry for 15 minutes, stirring as needed. Add the garlic and the dry spices, including the hawaij if using – an amazing aroma will fill your kitchen! - then let this fry for 5 minutes.

Add the aniseed spirit, turn the heat up to let the alcohol evaporate, then add the harissa and water. After a couple of minutes, add the tinned tomatoes and a pinch of sugar, then it all simmer for 10 to 15 minutes.

Sprinkle a little salt and pepper on the cod fillets to season them then gently place them on top of the stew. Sprinkle half of the coriander on top. Pop the lid on and simmer for 5 minutes.

Take the lid off and add a good squeeze of lemon juice to the pot. Give the stew a good shake, taste to check the seasoning and then add the rest of the coriander.

Take the steaming pot to the table and let everyone dive in.

Serve with steaming rice and some lovely green veg. Enjoy!

> **"Human rights start with breakfast."**
> - Leopold Sedar Senghor

Crispy Roasted Chicken Legs with Couscous

Middle Eastern spiced to make them sing!

You will need a casserole pot that can go first on the hob and then into the oven

The punchy flavours on these chicken legs are amazing, served with the most delicious couscous. This dish will definitely fire up your taste buds!

INGREDIENTS

Serves 4
- 4 chicken legs
- 3 long shallots or 5 small ones, peeled and halved
- 2 tbsp olive oil

For the marinade
- 1 tbsp dried mint
- 1 tbsp za'atar spice mix
- 1 tbsp dried chilli flakes
- 1 tsp sea salt
- 3 tbsp pomegranate molasses
- 2 tbsp olive oil

For the couscous
- 200g couscous
- 3 spring onions, finely sliced
- 3 tbsp chopped coriander
- 25g walnuts, roughly chopped

METHOD

Mix all the ingredients for the marinade together to make a thick paste.

Make two or three long slashes on each of the chicken legs, then cover them all over with the paste by rubbing it on.

Put them in the fridge to marinate for at least 1 hour, or overnight if you prefer.

When you are ready to cook, preheat the oven to 200°c. Put the olive oil into the casserole and fry the shallots until they are lightly browned.

Then add the marinated chicken and transfer the pan to the oven, uncovered, and cook for 30 to 40 minutes until the chicken is cooked through and the skin is lovely and crispy.

While the chicken is cooking, prepare the couscous. Cook according to the instructions on the packet, which should take about 12 to 15 minutes and try to time it well so the chicken and couscous are ready at the same time.

When the chicken is cooked, remove the legs from the pan and then pour the cooking juices into the couscous. Stir in the spring onions, fresh coriander and walnuts until well combined. Serve the couscous with the chicken legs.

This works well with the tomato and pomegranate salad, or just some sliced tomatoes simply drizzled with olive oil.

Slow Roasted Middle Eastern Lamb

With Crushed Peas, Broad Beans and Feta

INGREDIENTS

Serves 4

- 4 tbsp olive oil
- 1½ lemons, juiced
- 2 tsp ground cumin
- 2 tsp fennel seeds
- 1 tsp ground coriander
- 1 tsp ground cardamom
- 1 tsp hot paprika
- 1 tsp chilli powder
- 4 cloves of garlic, crushed
- Bunch of coriander, finely chopped (leave some whole for garnish)
- 1kg lamb neck fillets
- 200g broad beans
- 200g peas
- 50g crumbled feta cheese
- Handful of mint, finely chopped (leave some whole for garnish)
- 50ml Greek yoghurt

METHOD

Combine half the olive oil with the juice of 1 lemon, the ground cumin, fennel seeds, ground coriander, ground cardamon, paprika, chilli powder, crushed garlic and fresh coriander. Add the lamb fillets to this marinade, cover the meat thoroughly and leave in the fridge for at least 4 hours, or overnight.

Preheat the oven to 160°c then put the lamb in a roasting dish and cover well. It's probably a good idea to use two

layers of foil to keep the meat lovely and moist. The lamb needs to be slow cooked for 2 to 2½ hours. Check after a couple of hours and if the meat falls apart when pulled with a fork it is ready. The outer crust should be a little crispy and golden.

Meanwhile, cook the peas and broad beans (the broad beans will need to be podded after cooking) then put them in a dish with the remaining lemon juice and olive oil, the crumbled feta, mint and some salt and pepper to taste. Crush this mixture with a masher but not until completely smooth as it still needs to have some texture.

Put the lamb on a board and pull it apart with two forks. Pile the feta and pea mixture on the side and put the yoghurt in a small dish to serve. Sprinkle with a few mint and coriander leaves and serve with flatbreads.

Hawaij Spice Mix

Amazing rub/spice mix

Always great to have in the cupboard to rub on chicken or fish for grilling or barbecuing.

INGREDIENTS

- 4 tbsp black peppercorns
- 4 tbsp cumin seeds
- 1 tbsp cardamon seeds (from the pods) or 1 tsp ground cardamon
- 2 tbsp ground turmeric
- 1 tsp cloves
- 2 tbsp coriander seeds, toasted

METHOD

To make the spice mix, heat a dry pan over a medium heat, add the spices then toast for 2 to 3 minutes. Grind all of them in a spice grinder or a pestle and mortar until they become a fine powder.

Store in airtight container. It will keep for 2 months.

"Shooting a smile into the air can help
lift the spirits of anyone who catches it."

"There is no greater satisfaction than
to do something special for someone
who cannot repay you."

Refugee Support - Aid with Dignity

Your attitude - your choice

Henry's Story

Henry is an only child from Lagos, Nigeria. He is a talented footballer and played with the national youth team for 3 years before he fled.

On the situation with Nigeria he says: "in Nigeria there are no human rights, no women's rights, you cannot do anything without corruption. No rights for people at all".

He has been in Greece for 18 months, spent one year in Moira camp in Lesvos and six months in Katsikas. "I cannot stay here, I cannot work, I cannot marry, I cannot do anything here."

About Refugee Support he says: "You help us. You help to make us happy. We love everyone working here...you talk to us and we love you."

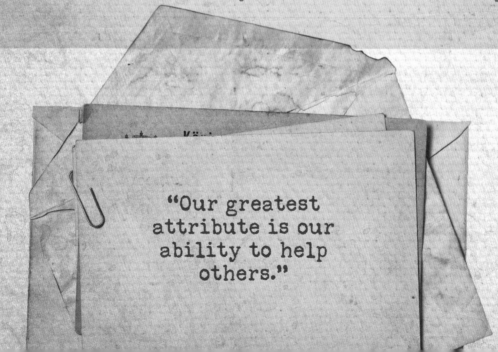

"Our greatest attribute is our ability to help others."

Fiery African Pepper Sauce

This sauce is so spicy, with such an African flavour. You need to use this very, very sparingly! It can be used as a dip, condiment or marinade.

If you don't want it to be so hot, reduce the amount of chilli peppers to a maximum of two.

INGREDIENTS

- 5 scotch bonnet peppers, deseeded and stems discarded
- 1 onion, roughly chopped
- 4 cloves of garlic, peeled and roughly chopped
- 1 vegetable stock cube, dissolved in 2 tbsp water
- 2 tbsp parsley
- 2 basil leaves
- 4 tomatoes, roughly chopped
- 50ml vegetable oil
- Salt

METHOD

Put all the ingredients except the salt into a food processor and blend.

Pour into a small saucepan and bring to the boil, then let it simmer for 15 minutes. Keep an eye on it, as you must take care it doesn't burn.

Taste carefully - it will be spicy - and then add salt to taste.

The sauce is now ready to serve hot or cold. You can store it in a screw top jar for a couple of weeks in the fridge.

"One of the most distressing aspects of a refugee's journey is that they are never sure when or where it is going to end."

"You can't shake hands with a clenched fist."
— Indira Gandhi

Berbere
Spice Mix

Great to have in a
jar ready to use. You
can throw it into any
dish to add some extra
flavour or rub on
chicken or lamb before
popping on the grill.

INGREDIENTS

- 60g dried chillies
- 30g paprika
- 1 tbsp cayenne pepper
- 1 tsp onion powder
- 1 tsp ground ginger
- 1 tsp ground cumin
- 1 tsp ground coriander
- 1 tsp ground cardamom
- 1 tsp fenugreek
- ½ tsp cinnamon
- 1 tsp ground allspice
- ½ tsp ground cloves

METHOD

Mix everything together - that's it!

It's not what
you look at

It's how you choose
to look at it

Zhoug Sauce

Easy peasy
lemon squeezy!

This sauce is really popular in Yemen, but also all over the
Middle East, adding a burst of flavour to loads of dishes.

INGREDIENTS

- 1–3 whole green chillies, sliced
- 2 fat cloves of garlic
- ½ tsp ground cardamom
- 1 tsp cumin
- ½ tsp chilli flakes
- ½ tsp salt
- 2 tbsp fresh lemon juice
- Bunch of coriander
- 80ml cup olive oil

METHOD

Put all the chillies, garlic, cardamom,
cumin, chilli flakes, salt, lemon juice
and coriander in a food processor
and blend until smooth.

Lastly, add the olive oil in a trickle
with the processor still running.

Tip: if you are wanting to
make this a day or two early,
it can be made in advance.
Just leave out the lemon
juice, adding that when you
are ready to use the sauce.

Kanafeh

Middle Eastern cheese and filo pastry dessert

INGREDIENTS

Serves 8
- 225g mozzarella, coarsely grated
- 140g cream cheese
- 450g filo pastry
- 340g butter, melted
- 320g caster sugar
- 1 lemon, juiced
- 1 tsp rose water
- 100g pistachios, chopped

METHOD

You will need a 10cm metal flan dish.

Preheat the oven to 200°c. Mix the cheeses together in a large bowl.

Shred the filo pastry into 1cm wide strips and then cut across them so they are about 2cm long.

Put the filo into a separate bowl and pour the melted butter over it.

Toss the butter with the filo and rub with your hands, taking your time to make sure each piece is covered.

Put half of the filo into the flan dish and press down with your fingers to make sure the whole base is covered and the pastry is evenly spread out.

Add the cheese mixture and spread it out evenly but don't go right up to the edges, leave about 1cm all round.

Scatter the rest of the filo on top of the cheese mixture, again spreading the pastry out evenly and pressing down with your fingers to achieve a firm flat top.

Place into the oven and cook for about 40 minutes until it is a deep golden brown colour.

Meanwhile, prepare the syrup. Put the sugar, lemon juice and 250ml water into a medium saucepan. Simmer until the sugar dissolves. It is ready when you can drop a small amount into iced water and it forms a soft ball. At this point, take the pan off the heat and stir in the rose water.

When the pie is ready, remove it from the oven and pour half the syrup over the top.

Then turn the pie upside down onto the serving platter and pour the rest of the syrup over it.

Sprinkle on the chopped pistachios and your kanafeh is ready to serve.

EQUAL RIGHTS FOR OTHERS DOES NOT MEAN LESS RIGHTS FOR IT IS NOT A PIE!

Yasmin's Cafe

One of the highlights of any volunteer's trip to the Katiskas camp in Greece was to be invited into Yasmin's cabin for an authentic home-cooked Syrian lunch.

Yasmin and her family had made the long and arduous journey from Syria to seek safety in Europe. Her passion was to cook and with the help of her son she would prepare the most amazing food once a week for the Refugee Support volunteers, treating all of us to 'a special taste of her distant homeland'. The food was gorgeous, and always tasted so much better when shared with such a wonderfully diverse mixture of people and cultures.

Yasmin had tried to establish her own cafe in the camp to help provide a little extra for her family, but this positive initiative was unfortunately quashed by the authorities.

Nutty Pista- chio Baklava

These golden nutty pastries soaked in sugar syrup are totally irresistible.

INGREDIENTS
Serves 8
- 200g pistachios, toasted
- 50g walnuts
- 50g blanched almonds
- 50g brown sugar
- ½ tsp ground cinnamon
- 200g butter, melted
- 270g filo pastry

For the syrup
- 250g caster sugar
- 200ml water
- 50g honey
- 1 tsp vanilla extract
- ½ lemon, juiced
- 1 cinnamon stick, broken into pieces
- 1 cardamom pod, squashed with the side of a knife

METHOD
Blitz the nuts in a food processor until they are in small pieces, but be careful not to overdo this as you don't want them to become a paste. Transfer into a bowl then mix in the brown sugar and ground cinnamon. Set to one side.

Brush the sides and base of a square 21cm by 21cm tin with the melted butter and then cut the first pack of filo pastry sheets in half so that they will fit in the tin. Put one sheet in the tin and brush with the melted butter, do the same with the second sheet, brushing again with butter and then keep layering like this

until you have used up half of the pastry. Tip the nut mixture onto the pastry and press it down to make it an even layer. Cut the second lot of pastry in half and layer them in the same way on top of the nut mixture, brushing each sheet with melted butter. When the baklava is assembled, pour the remaining butter over the top. Put the tin in the fridge to chill for 30 minutes or so.

Preheat the oven to 180°c. Take the tin out of the fridge and use a sharp knife to cut deep lines in the pastry, marking the baklava into small squares. Pop into the oven and bake for 20 minutes, then turn the oven down to 130°c for a further 30 minutes. The baklava should be lovely and golden brown. Remove it from the oven but leave it in the tin when done.

While the baklava is cooking, put all the ingredients for the syrup into a saucepan. Bring it to the boil and then turn the heat down low and let it simmer for around 10 minutes until the sugar has completely dissolved and the syrup is the consistency of runny honey. Strain the liquid to remove the cinnamon stick and cardamon.

Pour the warm syrup all over the baklava and leave it to soak in for a few hours.

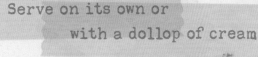

Serve on its own or with a dollop of cream

Crème Caramela

Sudanese Caramel Custard

This is one of Sudan's favourite puddings, and once you have tried it I am sure you will see why! It's very easy to eat the whole thing yourself, but really good to share.

INGREDIENTS

Serves 8
- 4 eggs
- 500ml milk
- 150g sugar
- 2 tsp vanilla extract
- 50g butter, melted
- 2 tbsp water

METHOD

Heat the oven to 180°c.

Beat the eggs with the milk and half of the sugar until frothy, then add the vanilla extract and set aside.

Put the rest of the sugar in a small frying pan and add 2 tablespoons of water. Heat slowly, stirring gently with a metal spoon until the sugar has dissolved (the base of the pan will no longer feel gritty when you run the

spoon over it). Increase the heat and allow the syrup to bubble, but DO NOT STIR AT ANY TIME from this point on. The bubbles will get bigger and the syrup will become thicker.

Watch the caramel very carefully and once it starts to turn golden, swirl the pan to ensure it colours evenly.

Once it has become a rich golden colour, remove the pan from the heat and either pour the caramel into a pudding bowl or divide it between eight ramekins. Briefly beat the egg mixture again and then quickly pour it on top of the caramel.

Cover the top of the bowl or ramekins with silver foil that has been well buttered. Place the bowls or ramekins into a large roasting tin that has been half filled with water.

Bake in the preheated oven for 30 minutes, then test whether the crème caramela is cooked with a metal skewer, which will come out clean if it is done.

Allow to cool in the fridge for at least 4 hours. When you are ready for dessert, turn out the crème caramela onto a platter, or individual plates, and serve.

Women's craft
centre, Cyprus

Siri's Story

Siri is a refugee from Nigeria, forced
to leave after his whole family was
slaughtered. In Libya he was enslaved
and tortured. From there he paid
traffickers to take him to Europe.
He is now in Nicosia, Cyprus, where
he sleeps on the streets. He has no
possessions and often days pass
without food.

Siri is just one of thousands in
the same situation. He is still a gentle
soul but if you look into his eyes, they
are empty.

There are only two small refugee
camps in Cyprus. They are isolated,
overcrowded and lacking in any level of
maintenance. The two camps can only
shelter a few hundred people but there
are up to 15,000 refugees currently
seeking refuge in Cyprus and the
authorities are totally overwhelmed by
the scale of the problem.

Food is provided at the camps,
but is of poor quality, and insufficient
in quantity.

In June 2019, Refugee Support set up
a dignity centre in the heart of Nicosia
that offers a whole menu of 'aid with
dignity' to refugees like Siri from all
corners of this troubled world.

West African Fruit Salad

It's very simple, but the lime and brown sugar dressing on this fresh salad really makes the fruit sing!

INGREDIENTS

Serves 4

- 1 pineapple
- 2 mangoes
- 2 bananas
- 3 oranges
- 1 lime, juiced
- 2 tbsp brown sugar
- Few mint leaves, chopped

METHOD

Peel and chop all the fruit into bite-size pieces and segment the orange so there is no membrane at all. Mix the lime juice and sugar together in a small jug.

Put the fruit into a large serving bowl and then add the dressing. Toss it through so that all the fruit is covered with the lime and sugar (hands work best for this).

Leave the salad somewhere cool to marinate for at least 1 hour, then sprinkle on the mint leaves and serve with some ice cream. Coconut ice cream works well.

Chocolate and Cardamom Tart

This rich Middle Eastern inspired tart is easy to make and looks stunning, and with the tantalising hint of cardamom it tastes just sublime! You can make your own sweet pastry or use a ready-made one as we have done below.

INGREDIENTS

Serves 8

- 300ml double cream
- 50g butter
- 200g dark chocolate, broken into squares
- 50g pistachos, chopped (plus a handful extra for decoration)

- Seeds from 8 cardamom pods
- 1 tsp rosewater
- 25cm sweet pastry case
- Small handful of dried apricots, roughly chopped (optional)
- Sprinkle of rose petals

METHOD

Put the cream and the butter into a saucepan on a very low heat just until the butter has melted, then take the pan off the heat. The mixture must not start to boil at this stage.

Quickly add the dark chocolate to the pan and stir as quickly and vigorously as you can until all the chocolate has melted. If the chocolate won't completely melt, you can pop it back on the heat, but just for a few seconds at a time to make sure it doesn't overheat.

Add the pistachios, cardamom seeds and rosewater to the chocolate filling.

The mixture should be lovely and glossy, so you can now pour it into the pastry case and smooth it over with a knife.

Sprinkle over the chopped apricots if using, the remaining pistachios and the rose petals.

The tart needs to cool for at least 2 hours before serving, so can easily be made the day before you need it. Keep the tart in the fridge until you need it.

This is lovely served with poached apricots, or just some ice cream or double cream on the side.

Iranian Carrot and Almond Cake

Moist, crumbly and full of goodness, it's only a little bit naughty!

INGREDIENTS

Serves 8
- 3 large eggs
- 200g caster sugar
- 2 tsp vanilla extract
- 200g ground almonds
- 70g desiccated coconut
- 2 tsps ground cinnamon
- 150g butter, melted
- 2 large carrots, coarsely grated
- 70g pistachio nuts, roughly chopped

METHOD

You will need a 23cm springform cake tin, with the sides and base greased or lined.

Preheat the oven 160°c. Crack the eggs into a large mixing bowl, add the sugar and vanilla extract and mix together well.

Add the almonds, coconut and cinnamon and stir everything together before adding the melted butter. Mix well. Then add the carrots and pistachios and mix again.

Tip the mixture into the cake tin and bake in the preheated oven for around 40 minutes, or until it is firm to the touch and has a crust on the top.

When the cake is ready take it out of the oven and leave to cool in the tin.

After it has cooled, sprinkle over some icing sugar or caster sugar to decorate and turn out onto a serving plate.

Serve with a dollop of ice cream and enjoy!

"EVERY life deserves
a certain amount of dignity
no matter how poor or
damaged the shell that
carries it."

– Refugee Support
Aid with Dignity

Somalian Almond Biscuits

These crunchy, nutty, buttery little biscuits are served in every cafe and house in Somalia. They are quick and easy to make and disappear very quickly!

INGREDIENTS

- 260g plain flour
- 130g sugar
- 130g ground almonds
- 230g butter, melted
- 1 tsp ground cardamom

METHOD

Preheat the oven to 175°c.

Line a baking tray with non-stick baking paper and brush with a little of the melted butter.

Mix all the dry ingredients together in a large bowl.

Make a well in the centre and pour in the melted butter then bring the

mixture together with your hands (if the dough needs more binding, add a little milk).

Roll some dough in your hand to make a golf ball sized ball and then flatten this into a disc shape.

Repeat until all the dough has been used up, leaving space between them on the baking tray as they will expand while baking.

Bake in the oven for 15 to 20 minutes until golden brown.

Put the biscuits on a wire rack and leave to cool for a while before serving.

Treacherous Crossing

Somalis risk death, rape, arbitary detention, forced labour and starvation as they travel towards the Mediterranean.

Held captive by gun-toting smugglers at a warehouse in southern Libya, newlywed Somali refugee Maryam was taken from her husband Ahmed and raped, repeatedly, over several months. Only when she became pregnant was she returned to him.

"They forced him to work and punished him in front of me to humiliate him,'" she says of the couple's ordeal, which was only just beginning.

"They continued to beat me despite my condition, but one day a smuggler pushed me very hard. I fell and I miscarried my baby."

After paying a ransom of 2,000 dinars (about £1000) they were freed, only to be betrayed and sold on to smugglers in the desert town of Bani Walid, by a local man who had promised to help them.

"Bani Walid was even worse than before. It was more painful. They would torture and punish my husband all the time. They even stabbed him in the thigh. I was raped again... again I fell pregnant... and again, due to the conditions there, I lost my baby."

One night a guard left a door unlocked and the couple seized their chance to finally escape. Sheltered by the Somali community in Tripoli, the couple later attempted to cross the Mediterranean. But, like so many others, they were intercepted by the authorities and returned to Ain Zara detention centre in Tripoli.

Thousands of refugees and migrants risk their lives in the hands of traffickers and smugglers on dangerous journeys from sub-Saharan Africa to North Africa, many seeking to reach safety in Europe.

Dangers along the route include being kidnapped, murdered, raped or sexually assaulted, being left to die in the desert, or being sold as slaves. Of those who reach the shores of the Mediterranean aboard a boat, at least 331 people died or went missing at sea in 2019 after departing Libya, a rate equivalent to about one in six who attempt the journey.

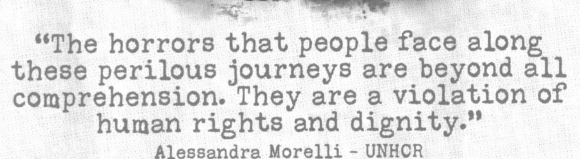

"The horrors that people face along these perilous journeys are beyond all comprehension. They are a violation of human rights and dignity."

Alessandra Morelli - UNHCR

West African Fresh Ginger Cake

Our Uncle David, 89, is famous for making his legendary ginger cake. He has made one a week for 40 years to share with friends and family, and anyone he thinks could do with a little extra love. I was a bit sceptical that a different recipe could live up to Uncle David's secret recipe, but I have to say this one is delicious!

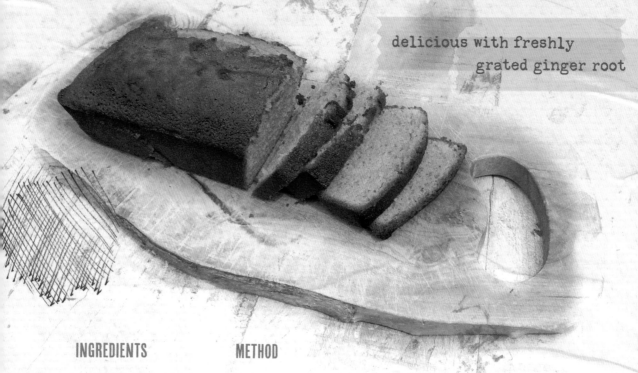

delicious with freshly grated ginger root

INGREDIENTS

- 160g plain flour
- 1 tsp baking powder
- 1 tsp ground ginger
- ½ tsp ground cinnamon
- ¼ tsp salt
- 130g unsalted butter, softened
- 110g caster sugar
- 110g brown sugar
- 2 large eggs
- 2cm fresh ginger root, grated
- ½ tsp vanilla extract
- 125ml fresh milk

METHOD

Preheat the oven to 180°c and grease a loaf tin.

Put the flour, baking powder, ground ginger, cinnamon and salt in a bowl and mix together.

Cream the butter and both types of sugar together in a separate large bowl.

Add the eggs, grated ginger and vanilla extract to the butter and sugar. Carefully add the milk, trying not to let it curdle.

Stir in the flour mixture until everything is totally combined. A manual hand-held whisk is good for this.

Pour the mixture into the prepared tin and bake in the oven for around 40 minutes. You can tell if it's ready by seeing if a skewer comes out clean.

Leave the cake in the tin for about 10 minutes to cool and then turn it out onto a serving plate, slice and enjoy.

Refugee Support Dignity Centre, Cyprus

In June 2019 the first RS Dignity Centre opened in Nicosia, Cyprus, providing friendship, help and support to refugees and displaced people.

The Dignity Centre has helped to provide refugees with a real sense of community and purpose. The centre is evolving but is already providing education and language classes to both children and adults.

The children's play groups not only give the kids added stimulation, but allows the women to attend sewing, craft and cookery sessions, while the men are busy in the cycle repair workshop.

The impact and positivity this fantastic project has had on the refugees in Cyprus is simply incredible.

The most beautiful items are being made, with 70% of the profits being paid directly to the refugee maker.

Learn more at refumade.org

181

Poached Syrian Apricots in Ginger Wine with Pistachios and Ricotta

The perfect happy ending to a Middle Eastern feast.

INGREDIENTS

- 500ml ginger wine
- 3 tbsp brown sugar
- 8 ripe apricots
- 250g ricotta
- 100g yoghurt
- 3 tbsp honey
- Handful of pistachios, roughly chopped

METHOD

Put the ginger wine and the sugar into a large saucepan, and slowly bring to the boil.

Stir gently to dissolve the sugar totally, and then continue to simmer for 10 minutes.

Add the apricots, make sure they are covered by the liquid and then simmer gently for 3 to 5 minutes or until the apricots are just tender.

Take the apricots out of the pan and put them into a bowl. Increase the heat under the saucepan and simmer until the liquid has reduced and is thick and syrupy. This will take around 30 minutes.

Pour the syrup over the apricots and leave in the fridge to cool.

Put the ricotta and yoghurt in a bowl and whisk them together, then add the honey and mix again before folding in the pistachios.

To serve, put a couple of apricots in individual small bowls with some of the syrup and add a spoonful of the ricotta mixture to each.

Scrumptious Glazed and Grilled Pineapple Slices

INGREDIENTS

- 1 fresh pineapple, peeled
- 4 tbsp butter
- 1 tbsp brown sugar
- 1 tsp cinnamon

METHOD

Preheat the grill or barbecue while you slice the pineapple into 1cm rings.

Melt the butter in the microwave, which should only take about 20 seconds, then add the sugar and cinnamon and mix well.

Dip the pineapple rings into the glaze and cover completely.

Place each ring on the grill or barbecue. Turn over after about 3 or 4 minutes, once the side facing the grill is golden, and repeat on the other side. Serve hot.

So good, and so easy - serve with a lovely ball of ice cream.

Sweet, sticky and scrumptious - you won't believe how good these are!

"Refugees are part of humanity and we cannot leave them behind."

- Ger Duany

Mutaki
Syrian Walnut and Cardamom Cookies

Blink and they are gone, because these cookies are delicious!

INGREDIENTS

- 200g plain flour
- ¼ tsp baking powder
- ¼ tsp salt
- 80g unsalted butter, chilled then cut into 1cm dice
- 60ml soured cream
- ¼ tsp vanilla extract
- 100g walnut pieces
- 50g caster sugar
- 50g currants
- ½ tsp ground cardamom
- 2 large eggs, separated
- Icing sugar, for dusting

METHOD

Put half of the flour into a bowl with the baking powder and salt then stir to combine them.

Add the butter and rub the mixture through your fingers to create a fine breadcrumb-like texture.

Add the soured cream, vanilla extract, 2 tablespoons of water and the remaining flour. Mix well to form a soft dough.

Form a ball of dough then knead this on a floured work surface for 1 minute or so. Split the dough into 2 evenly sized pieces, cover with cling film and chill in the fridge for around 2 hours.

"Learn to appreciate the simple things."

While the dough rests, make the filling.

Put the walnuts into a food processor and pulse into small crumbs. Transfer these into a bowl, add the sugar, currants, cardamom and egg whites then stir to combine everything.

Take the chilled dough out of the fridge and roll one piece out as thinly as you can, then cut into squares of about 8cm.

Put a teaspoon of filling in one of the corners and then roll up the square as if you were making a croissant.

Repeat this for each square, and then repeat with the other ball of dough.

You should have 20 biscuits.

Put them onto baking sheets, leaving an inch between each one.

Put the egg yolks into a small bowl and beat them. Brush each of the cookies with this egg wash and then put them in the oven until golden. This should take about 20 minutes.

Put them on a wire rack to cool and then dust with icing sugar before serving.

Refugee Support
Free Shop
Aid with Dignity

She explains that "there have been days, months when I've eaten meals provided by charities, governments, and good people.

In total these days have made up a sliver of my life and yet, after decades of eating well and returning favours, I struggle to accept a cup of coffee."

"The Refugee Support shop Paul and John opened is a well designed, peaceful marketplace where a person of note wouldn't be ashamed to shop. They decided to display the goods and give the people the respect of choosing."

Camp residents shop for essential goods in the same way we all do, using the currency of points issued weekly by Refugee Support, selecting items for themselves and their families and at the same time stopping to chat with the volunteers in the shop and their fellow camp residents.

One of the very best examples of how Refugee Support delivers on its pledge to provide refugees with not simply support but 'aid with dignity' is the Free Shop concept.

This idea came to Refugee Support founders John Sloan and Paul Hutchings when volunteering in Calais, where they helped hand out food and clothing from the back of a van.

They both felt that although the refugees were grateful and understood the kindness of the people who were giving, the way it was done was insensitive and humiliating for the refugees.

This resonated well with Dina Nayeri (author of The Ungrateful Refugee). Dina was herself a refugee and understands the loss of dignity, humiliation and shame that can be felt by refugees accepting charity.

Refugee Support Volunteers

So many of us look on helplessly at the plight of the many thousands of refugees fleeing from conflicts across the world with no safe place to go.

Refugee Support is an amazing independent NGO that unconditionally provides a unique form of aid with dignity.

Offering your time to be a Refugee Support Volunteer is such a rewarding and humbling experience. It is open to anyone of any age or background.

Go on, do it - you won't regret it!

Find out more about how to become a volunteer at www.refugeesupporteu.com

"Refugee children have lost their homes.

But we cannot allow them to lose their future."

Refugee Support Europe

John Sloan and
Paul Hutchings,
co-founders

They set out with a vision for the world where all refugees can live a life with dignity.

In 2016 they set up Refugee Support Europe. This small, dynamic organization has achieved so much under John and Paul's leadership, and with the support of passionate volunteers, they are successfully delivering their goal of providing 'Aid with Dignity' wherever they can.

www.refugeesupport.eu

INDEX

Almond
Iranian carrot and almond cake 176
Somalian almond biscuits 178

Apple
West African fruit salad 172

Apricot
Poached apricots in ginger wine 182

Asparagus
Asparagus, broad bean
and garlic salad 64

Aubergine
Baba ganoush 8
Roasted aubergine and pepper salad 20
Grilled aubergine with harissa
and yoghurt 42

Avocado
Fattoush salad with avocado 68

Bananas
West African fruit salad 172

Beef
Iranian beef skewers 32

Beetroot
Beetroot and yoghurt dip 6

Broad Bean
Broad bean hummus 16
Broad bean salad 54
Asparagus, broad bean and
garlic salad 64

Bulgar Wheat
Tabbouleh 58
Middle Eastern roasted salmon with
chickpea couscous 148

Butternut Squash
Roasted and spiced
butternut squash 66

Cabbage
African cabbage salad 70

Carrots
African cabbage salad 70
Roasted spiced carrots 72
Sweet potato, carrot, lentil
and spinach curry 90
African vitality burger 128
Iranian carrot and almond cake 176

Cauliflower
Whole Middle Eastern cauliflower 52
Cauliflower and chickpea tagine 82

Chicken
Iranian chicken kebabs 30
Ethopian chicken stew, doro wat 78
Chicken shawarma 88
Chicken satay 92
African chicken wings 94
African one pot spicy
chicken peanut stew 98
Middle Eastern herb and
garlic chicken 100
Middle Eastern chicken
and rice 102
Yassa chicken 108
Irqai chicken and rice 116
Chicken and potato curry 134

Somalian peri peri chicken 138
Spicy chicken with harissa
and lentils 142
Crispy roasted chicken legs
with couscous 154

Chickpeas
Hummus 16
Broad bean hummus 16
Cauliflower and chickpea tagine 82
Middle Eastern fish stew 112
African vitality burger 128
Middle Eastern roasted salmon with
chickpea couscous 148

Chillies
Fiery African pepper sauce 160
Zhoug sauce 164

Chocolate
Chocolate and cardamom tart 174

Coconut Milk
Somalian peri peri chicken 138
West African shrimp 144

Cod
Middle Eastern fish stew 112
Fish chraymeh 152

Courgette
Courgette, feta and herb fritters 40
Grilled courgettes 44
Middle Eastern courgettes 48
African vitality burger 128
Middle Eastern roasted salmon with
chickpea couscous 148
Crispy roasted chicken legs
with couscous 154

Crème cheese

Kanafeh - Middle Eastern cheese
and filo pastry **166**

Cucumber

Mast o khiar - Persian
yoghurt dip **12**

Eggs

Kuku sabzi - Persian
herb frittata **36**
Shakshuka **38**
Turkish menemem scrambled eggs **50**
Creme caramela **170**
West African ginger cake **180**

Feta Cheese

Persian marinated feta **28**
Courgette, feta and herb fritters **40**

Filo Pastry

Kanefeh - Middle Eastern cheese
and filo pastry desert **166**
Pistachio nutty baklava **168**

Fish

Cameroon roasted fish **106**
Middle Eastern fish stew **112**
Grilled salmon with North
African flavours **114**
Herb and nut crusted salmon **126**
Fish chraymeh **152**

Ginger

West African ginger cake **180**

Kale

Vegan peanut, sweet potato and
kale stew **136**

Lamb

Middle Eastern lamb koftas
with pistachios **34**
Roasted lamb koftas **88**
Ghomeh sabzi, Persian herb stew **121**
Barbecued whole leg of lamb **130**
Slow roasted Middle Eastern lamb **156**

Lentils

Lentil soup **22**
Mejadra, Arabic rice
with lentils **76**
Sweet potato, carrot, lentil
and spinach curry **90**
Spicy chicken with harissa
and lentils **142**

Lettuce

Middle Eastern green salad **56**
Fattoush salad with avocado **68**

Mackerel

Cameroon roasted fish **106**

Monkfish

Kuwaiti fish stew **84**

Mushroom

Bangledeshi mushroom and
pea curry **150**

Pastry

Chocolate and cardamom tart **174**

Peanut Butter

Chicken satay **92**
African one pot spicy
chicken peanut stew **98**
African vitality burger **128**

Peanuts

Vegan peanut, sweet potato and
kale stew **136**

Peas

Bangladeshi mushroom and
pea curry **150**

Peppers

Muhammara - Syrian red
pepper dip **10**

Pineapple

West African fruit salad **172**
Grilled and glazed pineapple slices **182**

Pomegranate

Tomato and pomegranate salad **60**

Potato

Whole roasted potatoes **104**
Hara batara - Middle
Eastern skillet potatoes **132**
Chicken and potato curry **134**

Prawns

Prawns alla busara **80**
West African shrimp **144**

Rice

Middle Eastern courgettes **48**
Majedra - Arabic rice
and lentils **76**
Middle Eastern chicken
and rice **102**
Iraqi chicken and rice **116**
Jewelled rice **122**
Cameroon vegetable
jollof rice **146**

Salmon

Grilled salmon with North African flavours **114**

Herb and nut crusted salmon **126**

Middle Eastern roasted salmon with chickpea couscous **148**

Spices

Hawaij spice mix **158**

Berbere spice mix **162**

Spinach

Spinach and herb soup **24**

Sweet potato, carrot, lentil and spinach curry **90**

Split Peas

Split pea and vegetable soup **26**

Sweet Potato

Sweet potato, carrot, lentil and spinach curry **90**

Vegan peanut, sweet potato and kale stew **136**

Tomato

Tomato and pomegranate salad **60**

Bangladeshi mushroom and pea curry **150**

Vegetarian (vegan*)

Iranian carrot and almond cake **176**

Somalian almond biscuits **178**

West African fruit salad* **172**

Poached apricots in ginger wine **182**

Asparagus, broad bean & garlic salad* **64**

Baba ganoush* **8**

Roasted aubergine salad* **20**

Grilled aubergine with harissa and yoghurt **42**

Beetroot and yoghurt dip **6**

Broad bean hummus* **16**

Broad bean salad* **54**

Tabbouleh* **58**

Roasted and spiced butternut squash **66**

African cabbage salad* **70**

Roasted spiced carrots **72**

Sweet potato, carrot lentil and spinach curry* **90**

African vitality burger* **128**

Whole Middle Eastern cauliflower **52**

Cauliflower and chickpea tagine* **82**

Hummus* **16**

Zhoug sauce* **164**

Chocolate and cardamom tart **174**

Courgette, feta and herb fritters **40**

Grilled courgettes* **44**

Middle Eastern courgettes* **48**

Kanafeh, Middle Eastern cheese and filo pastry dessert **166**

Mast o khiar, Perisan yoghurt dip **12**

Kuku Sabzi, Persian herb frittata **185**

Shakshuka **36**

Turkish menemem scrambled eggs **50**

Creme caramela **170**

West African ginger cake **180**

Persian marinated feta **28**

Pistachio nutty baklava **168**

Peanut, sweet potato and kale stew* **136**

Lentil soup **22**

Mejadra - Arabic rice with lentils* **76**

Middle Eastern green salad **56**

Fattoush salad with avocado **68**

Bangladeshi mushroom and pea curry **150**

Grilled and glazed pineapple slices* **182**

Tomato and pomegranate salad* **60**

Whole roasted potatoes* **104**

Hara batara - Middle Eastern skillet potatoes **132**

Spinach and herb soup **24**

Walnuts

Mutaki - Syrian walnut and cardamom cookies **184**

Yoghurt

Mast o khiar - Perisan yoghurt salad **12**

Beetroot and yoghurt dip **6**